Praise for *Musings on Career and Faith*

"*Musings on Career and Faith* offers thoughtful insights for those inside and outside the boardroom. These brilliant and well-crafted reflections are simple yet profound, and ones for us to ponder as we respond to our higher calling of work.... There is simply something for everyone looking to maximize their influence as a leader."

—ALANA WALKER CARPENTER, CEO, Intriciti

"In his uncanny ability to draw you into each musing, Bates underscores our interconnectedness and our need to nourish our mind, body, and spirit. This book is a reminder to readers that we do not need to sacrifice our spiritual self for our work, but rather find a level of fulfillment in being our true self."

—DEENA KLODT (MICHIF), Red River Metis and Member of the Manitoba Metis Federation

"Paul eloquently articulates the dilemma of personal and professional self-actualization, giving real examples and sharing spiritual insights with solutions. Paul is intuitive, imaginative, and ingenuous in this delightful book, where each chapter name intrigues you and encourages you to continue to the next.... His words will chime an illuminating chord for many."

—JOSIE CASSANO RIZZUTI, Equity, Diversity, and Inclusion Lead, ArcelorMittal Dofasco

"Paul weaves all aspects of life into a seamless tapestry stitched with divine light, wisdom, and integrity. He opens his readers' eyes to the sacredness of work, the holiness of play, and the importance of living our values every day. Paul is a natural mentor. He ensures that people feel heard, seen, and prized. This shines through each of his musings, warming readers' souls and illuminating pathways of hope and possibility. That will be Paul's legacy."

—SUE-ANN WARD, Rector, Grace Anglican Church

"'Dear children, let us not love with words or tongue but with actions and in truth' (1 John 3:18). This theme underlines Paul's *Musings on Career and Faith* as he reflects on what he has learned in his journey of life. Foundational are the lessons learned on how one can have a fulfilling career while still honoring God. . . . Paul's book is a call to action for those willing to rise to the challenge."

—PAUL M. FIELD, retired Financial Services Executive

Musings on
Career and Faith

Musings on Career and Faith

PAUL K. BATES

WIPF & STOCK · Eugene, Oregon

MUSINGS ON CAREER AND FAITH

Wipf & Stock
An Imprint of Wipf and Stock Publishers
199 W. 8th Ave., Suite 3
Eugene, OR 97401

www.wipfandstock.com

PAPERBACK ISBN: 978-1-6667-3145-3
HARDCOVER ISBN: 978-1-6667-2396-0
EBOOK ISBN: 978-1-6667-2397-7

10/20/21

For Rachel, Elizabeth, and Charlotte

Contents

Contents

Contents

Author's Note

Some years ago a company that I held an executive position with was sold to another company in the same sector. Together with a number of our staff, I would personally not be staying on as our company was merged with the acquiring organization. As the transition unfolded a number of individuals were let go; usually on a Friday. The day came for the last group to leave, which included me. As I began to close my office, I received an email from another staff member who was scheduled to leave that final Friday also. He wrote, "Paul, don't be sorry that it's over; be happy that it happened."

Careers take new directions. Turning points remind us of the gifts we receive.

This book is written, with love, for every person who is both striving to do their best in life, and in so doing, is searching also for life's deepest meaning. The lessons are those that I have learned myself, and tried to share with others. It is about the journey, it is about the lessons learned, and it is about faith.

Makaroi: persons characterized by transcendent happiness or religious joy: blessed, happy.

Introduction

I have been a businessperson, a public servant, a teacher, a volunteer, a student, a pastor, a husband, a father, and a grandfather. Fifty years ago, I turned away from faith. Thirty years ago, I returned.

I hope that there will be a few anecdotes that are inspiring and, perhaps, challenging for you in this little book, which I begin with the final words of Dr. Jay Lombard in his engaging work, *The Mind of God: Neuroscience, Faith, and a Search for the Soul.* He writes, "God knits us human beings together in love. It is a memory that goes back to the creation of the universe. And it is in love that we live forever."[1] Love is a *binding* agent. Love implies a *co-dependency*, and co-dependency implies mutual obligation. Love must be held fast; hatred must be tossed away.

As I think about it, you may wish to have your Bible with you as you read this book as there are several references that you may wish to explore.

Work comes in all forms. Perhaps most fundamental is the work of keeping a home. I'm not sure that she realized that I was paying attention, but my mother taught me the fundamentals of fiduciary behavior—although she would never have used that term. She also taught me to cook. We were a post-war, working-class family, and my mother knew how to make the most of our ration books, together with the modest income that she earned toward the family budget in whatever way that she could she could; from hand-painting toy soldiers, to stringing together faux-pearl jewelry, to serving as a housekeeper and shopkeeper. One of my earliest memories was Bubble and Squeak—a side dish that you looked forward to the day after a meal that included potatoes and various other vegetables:

1. Lombard, *Mind of God,* 179.

1

Brussels sprouts, cabbage, carrots, parsnips, you name it. You fry it all up, and then add it to your next meal! Real comfort food! Making the most of everything in a time of shortage was a critical lesson for me. Indeed, my father had a saying, "Any meal is a feast." This from someone who, although he never talked about it, likely missed a few meals.

During my life, although there have been some tight moments, we never missed a meal, for which I give thanks to God. My father's expression, though, has held many messages for me in terms of how to live without squandering. Some of them I learned and kept early. Some became clearer to me as I grew older. These messages, together with lessons I have learned from my mother and indeed all my family, together with many colleagues and co-workers over the years, I now understand more completely. These lessons have been interwoven with my theology studies—they all have come together to illuminate my path. They have shaped my purpose, and I am happy. Many of these lessons are offered to you here.

Jay Lombard asserts that our existence is made complete by our deep awareness and knowledge of our purpose. He writes:

> True freedom is a key to a seemingly locked door. We are all handed the key and invited to open the door. But it's our choice whether or not to progress. Once through the doorway, we find on the other side a wide and open expanse of possibility. We embrace true freedom; we are free to live the lives we were meant to live. We can live lives of real purpose.[2]

Lombard's use of the term "door" resonates with my own concept of a threshold—a *liminal* space—which I will discuss later. If you spend any time on a commuter train, and you sit in the non "quiet-zone" car, you will find yourself listening in to many conversations around you that seem to be at odds with Lombard's aspirational perspectives. As the work week wears on and at the end of the work day, many, if not most, of the conversations and telephone calls you will overhear are about disappointment or aggravation at work: dealing with a counterproductive, even inept supervisor, lack

2. Lombard, *Mind of God*, 113.

of appreciation, abusive treatment by a customer, exasperation with a co-worker, or worse. I seldom hear praise and appreciation. Is it supposed to be like this? From my studies, I am aware that from the earliest of the ancient Hebrew texts, all aspects of life were considered to be integral to a covenantal relationship with God (cf. Deut 6:4–9).

My spiritual reawakening began during the years in which I participated in a men's bible discussion group—meeting at 7 AM weekly in an office tower high above the trading desks of the financial district. This awakening eventually led to my studies in practical theology, in my case focussed on the exploration and discussion of divine purpose in our work, and how we might discover happiness as we recognize and understand that divine purpose for each of us.

As you read and contemplate the various "musings" herein, I hope you will find items that compel you to do your own research and expand your knowledge and views on the topics presented.

Decide to Be All in and You Will Never Run out of Energy

Martin Buber writes:

> When I confront a human being as my You and speak the basic word I-You to him, then he is no thing among things nor does he consist of things. He is no longer He or She, limited by other Hes and Shes, a dot in the world grid of space and time, nor a condition that can be experienced and described, a loose bundle of named qualities. Neighbour-less and seamless he is You and fills the firmament. Not as if there were nothing but he; but everything else lives in *his* light.[3]

What I believe Buber is saying, fundamentally, is that when we *see* another person as a whole human being, they *become* a whole person. *I invite you to try this as soon as you can.* When another

---

3. Buber, *I and Thou*, 59 (emphasis original).

person realizes that you have *seen* them, you are going to notice an extraordinary change in that person's entire demeanor. I tried this during a speech recently—I asked everyone to stand and look at someone at a distant table, and to notice what happened to that person when they realized that they had be seen. Their entire demeanor changed. In fully seeing others, I have *also* become a more complete person myself. I have become far more calm and patient. I have found that there is very little to get angry about, although, paradoxically, I am far more aware of bad behavior.

As you know so well, life at work is filled with highs and lows. At times we are uplifted, but occasionally we are misunderstood; sometimes ill-treated, or simply ignored. In this journey, I have learned to forgive. As the gospel of Luke admonishes us, "Be merciful, just as your Father is merciful."[4] I have also learned that forgiveness is required *regardless* of whether the person who is the subject of your forgiveness shows any sign of acknowledgment of their wrongdoing, let alone apology, or even simply changed behavior. There will be a number of examples in this book of my encouragement to be *all in*. The first is to be *all in* when it comes to investing in others: This is our greatest calling.

Dr. James Roche Verling

A few years ago, I was invited to deliver a paper at a conference in Limerick, Ireland. Having a day to myself, I took a bus from Limerick to Cork. Walking through this beautiful town I came across the story of Dr. James Roche Verling (1787–1858). After graduating in medicine from the University of Edinburgh, he became an army surgeon, serving on HMS Northumberland, which brought the captured Napoleon to St. Helena. Verling became the personal physician to Napoleon. He later returned to his family home in Cobh, where he is buried. What an extraordinary life. How I would have liked to have met him. I invite you to sit for a while and reflect on this person's

---

4. Luke 6:36. Unless otherwise noted, all Scripture references are taken from the New Revised Standard Version (NRSV).

journey in life—returning full circle after so many extraordinary adventures. When we learn of the life of a person, sometimes long after they lived, that person's contribution to society grows a little more.

On Shrinking

Here is another outcome of learning to *see whole people*. The people that we see, as they become *whole* in front us, take up space in our lives that we may have previously been at risk of filling with our own self-importance. In other words, we shrink in relative size—at least in terms of our own ego. This act of shrinking is not only a critical step toward personal authenticity, but it is, I believe, a critical element of the path to faith. It is a step toward letting go. Shrinking may also be the first step to *heroism*. Indeed, it occurs to me that no act of heroism involves self-interest; rather it is empathy that is the spark of heroism. Luke 10:25–37 recounts Jesus' parable of the good Samaritan—a story that captures empathy and the heroic response that follows. Carol Paukner was a police officer with the New York City Police Department Transit Division, District 2, Lower Manhattan, when the devastation of September 11, 2001 erupted. She is quoted to have said, "How could I leave all these people? I said to another officer, 'I'm going to die today.' I just looked at the building and said, 'This is my day.'"[5] Heroes are not filled with self-importance—they are filled with resoluteness and they are emptied of their self-importance.

Be Knowledgeable, Be Courteous, Be Quick

To succeed, we must be knowledgeable; we must be courteous; we must be quick! My mother grew into adulthood during a difficult

---

5. Haga and Carouba, *Women at Ground Zero*, 4.

time—in the dockland area of East London, England, during the Blitz (1940–41). At one point she had worked as a bus conductor on one of those iconic red double-decker buses. As I said earlier, she later took on many jobs, including as a shop clerk and, ultimately, shop manager. But here's the thing that I noticed as I became old enough to notice: she *threw* herself into every role. She learned everything there was to learn in order to excel in what she did; she showed up for work no matter what, and she offered deep respect for everyone that she worked with and for. She saw her work as important enough to give it everything she had, and she knew well her limitations. She went *all in*.

Fast forward a few decades and I found myself relatively newly installed in a leadership role in the investment industry when the events of October 19th, 1987 rocked global markets. The wrenching turmoil of those markets meant that our clients would be turning to us for answers. We made a decision that, all these decades later, still feels like it was the right action to have taken. We secured a full page in one of the major financial newspapers and we wrote a multihundred-word piece in which we presented our response and how investors might also respond. There was no "white space," as the ad agencies term it, just words. We threw ourselves into preparing this communication overnight. We relied on our collective knowledge, we showed deep respect for our clients, and we were careful not to step beyond that which we felt we understood. We went *all in*.

I am reminded of those events every time there is a jarring market inflection. I am reminded that it is crucial to have made sure that our team's and my own knowledge is deep and robust, so that when dramatic inflection moments occur, we can rely on that knowledge in order to respond. Further, we must be quick to transfer that knowledge to our clients. Finally, we must have the depth of courtesy that is required to ensure that our clients get exactly what they are asking for, whatever it takes.

And, when the turmoil subsides, we must take stock and examine ourselves and our actions thoroughly. Were we knowledgeable enough? Were we courteous enough? Were we quick enough? There is another lesson here. We must know our craft very well—so well that in a crisis we are able to act instinctively when there is no time to reach for the manual.

I learned this well during riding lessons. My instructor had me cross the stirrups across my horse's back, just in front of the saddle, and drop the reins on his withers, while she led my horse at the end of a lunge line at a trot, and then a canter. Later, when my horse chose to make a sharp turn right in front of a jump I stayed on. Thanks to my instructor's drills, my response was instinctive.

Seasons of Life

I have been doing something that I have never done before—I have been keeping a small journal. It began a new season for me. I don't do it every day, but writing in my journal has brought me more reflection than before. The Greek word καιροῖς, or *kairos*, is generally translated as "season." Looking back, I recognize the season that is midlife, experienced by many beginning in their early forties, can be interpreted as a form of passage—a shift from one state in life to another, often a significant shift. For many, their former state and its values may no longer be satisfying. Things may no longer make sense. This season has been described by some, initially, as disorienting and even debilitating, yet this season is also one of special opportunity—an extraordinary chance to truly flourish—from "getting by" to embarking on the creation of one's legacy. It can be, for many, a time of decisions and turning points. Indeed, I started a business at age forty-two. It was a turning point which shaped the rest of my career. This is the season also, perhaps, when the most important financial decisions of our lives are made. These are the decisions that will underpin and enable the rest of our lives. If we are serving clients who are in the season of midlife, it occurs to me that this is the time, more than ever, when we must ask to be invited into a deeper conversation—one that involves an understanding of aspirations, concerns, plans for new horizons and purpose—plans of legacy. This may be a time to broaden our network and deepen our community and volunteer work: a time to return favors.

Picture Your Hand in a Bucket of Water

Are you considering moving on but having difficulty letting go? Picture your hand in a bucket of water.

When is it time to move on in your career? Shortly before writing this, I received a call from a former student of mine. I cherish speaking with former students and getting updated on what is going on in their lives. In this case I was sorry to hear about the circumstance that my former student found himself in, but at the same time I felt privileged that he would call me to discuss it. The bottom line in terms of his situation was that while he was proud of the growth of the division of the business that he was responsible for, he was finding that he was going home at the end of the day with a heavy feeling that he was being forced to compromise in the way that he believed that others in the organization should be treated, based on his observation of the behavior of several of his superiors.

The nagging question of whether or not it is time to look for a new role, while triggered by a variety of events and situations, comes to most of us at some point. Often, we stay out of loyalty to one or two people. Sometimes we feel that the environment or business will suffer failure if we move on. Sometimes we are concerned that whatever we go to will be less financially rewarding than our current position. A respondent to a research questionnaire that I used for my doctoral research stated, "The industry changed and, in my view, became less ethical. I joined a small firm owned by a gay Christian man, who is on the same page as me in terms of ethics and purpose."[6]

Many years ago, I remember having a conversation with a colleague and mentor of mine named Stu. I was wrestling with the "Do I go or do I stay?" dilemma. I will never forget one of the points he made to me. He said, "Paul, picture your hand in a bucket of water. Now picture removing your hand from the water and ask yourself if there is a hole in the water where your hand was!" His sage comment was given to remind me that the world will go on without us, and that I should focus on seeking the right environment for me—one where I could fulfill my vocational aspirations in the most

---

6. Research respondent.

complete way possible. That said, the way we manage our separation in a way that is fair, honorable, and in keeping with our values, is important. *We are remembered for our behavior in times of change.* I have witnessed some who broke a lot of glass on the way out. Such is the wrong thing to be remembered for.

I also learned something else that is important here. In any employment situation, we are, in effect, either *borrowing reputation* from our employer, or we are *loaning reputation—our reputation—* to our employer. If the situation we are in feels constantly like the latter, it's probably time to move on.

In all things, we should give our best effort to our employer, but when the bargain no longer seems to be in equilibrium, it's time to dust off the CV.

Santa and the High Street Merchants

Let's remember what the High Street merchants taught us. How many of you watched the movie *Miracle on 34th Street* again this past holiday season? I had the chance to watch it (reluctantly at first, I admit it) with one of my grandchildren.

The central plot, of course, is the courtroom trial of a New York department store Santa Claus who claims that he is the *real* Santa Claus. There is a wonderful secondary plot that is the story of a little girl who, with the help of that same Santa Claus, nudges her mother toward a new romance with great promise for the future—a Christmas present indeed!

But I want to focus on a tertiary plot that unfolds. This Santa teaches the store clerks to send clients to other stores when those stores may have the right product for them—products that these same store clerks realize that they don't have in their own store. At first, the store's marketing department is aghast, until it takes the store president to realize its brilliance and makes it store policy. Here is a big-city department store doing what many small shop-owners have known all along. Go to any small town near you to test it out. Where I grew up most towns had what was known as the

High Street; the place to find the baker, the butcher, the florist, the hair dresser, the pharmacist, the bank, and so on.

These shop owners knew that they were part of the fabric of the community. Products were not SKUs, and customers were not simply buyers—they were neighbors. Stores were part of the vibrant and complex uniqueness that gave their village or town its identity. Everyone knew everyone's name, and everyone knew that word traveled fast! With every interaction, the right to do business was on the line, and so was the shop owner's reputation. Some interactions resulted in a transaction and some did not—indeed some should not, because the shop owner knew that they did not have the right product to satisfy their customer's needs on that particular day. So instead of automatically trying to "cross-sell" to a substitute, they guided the customer to another store that likely had the desired product. They knew that the customer would be back at the right time. Trust had been gained; reputation enhanced.

There's an underlying set of rules here, and they are all based on deep knowledge. Knowledge of our products—and our competitors'—is critical. We must listen carefully to understand the specific needs expressed to appreciate when a competitor's product is the right product to recommend.

Finally, of course, is the recognition of participation in a community, in full knowledge that not all acts of service will result in a transaction. This service, however, will always build reputation. Sometimes we need Santa to remind us.

Symmetry: It's a Pickle

Selling pickles: It's all about symmetry. I live in a farming community. A number of my students at the university live on crop farms. In a recent finance and ethics course I had the task of explaining the concept of ensuring symmetry in a financial transaction.

It turned out that one of my students grew pickling cucumbers, some of which were sold at the farm gate to people who stopped by. Here was the point that we discussed. A buyer asks how much for a half-bushel basket of pickles, and you tell them, "Our price is $25 per half-bushel, but I must point out that sometimes there may be one or two overripe pickles in there." This is symmetry of information—both you and the prospective buyer possess identical knowledge. But if you know that it is likely that there are one or two overripe pickles in the half-bushel basket, but you do not tell the prospective buyer, you have not given the entire picture, and this is asymmetry! In other words, full disclosure is the right way to ensure that both parties in a transaction have all the information.

When presented in this simple way, it is hard to understand why anyone would have trouble saying, "Of course I would ensure complete disclosure, and therefore assurance of full symmetry of information." So why is it so hard for some businesspeople, a minority to be sure, to avoid hiding the ball when it comes to committing to a duty of best interest in all client dealings?

In my early days in the investment industry, I was a commodities futures broker. My clients fell into two groups. One group were *sellers of risk*, who wished to assure themselves of a specific future price for their commodity. The other group were *buyers of risk*, who wished to speculate on the future price of a given commodity. Add to the equation that speculators could, in most cases, acquire a futures contract with a five percent value down-payment, and there is a serious risk of a loss that could exceed the ability of the speculator to cover. When opening an account for a speculator, I would spend several hours with the speculator and in some cases together with their spouse. The goal of this sometimes-lengthy meeting, which was followed by signed agreements, was to ensure full and total disclosure and understanding of potential losses, and how mechanisms like margin calls and forced closure of an open position would work. With such transparency in place, I could act on behalf of the client.

The Narrow Gate

Jesus said, "Enter through the narrow gate; for the gate is wide and the road is easy that leads to destruction, and there are many who take it. For the gate is narrow and the road is hard that leads to life, and there are few who find it."[7] My final steps into faith involved repetitive, daily readings of Matthew 5–7: Matthew's account of the Sermon on the Mount. These chapters, wherein Jesus essentially laid out all of his instructions for a life in faith, have held my attention ever since. When I am feeling stressed or unsure, I seem always to end up coming back to these pages of Scripture. Jesus' instructions are fairly easy to interpret—though they may be challenging to follow.

Turning to Hebrew Scripture, the fourth book of the Torah is the book of Numbers. Known in some Jewish circles as "In the Wilderness," this ancient text serves an important role as it narrates the transition from an enslaved people who fled Egypt to the new generation that stood on the brink of the promised land. The book of Numbers presents the reader with a vision of new beginnings and of hope; hope in the wilderness. When we are in the wilderness, hope is *our* beacon also.

There are many who have wandered in the desert. It is a place we must wrestle, frequently alone, with the changes we must make, if we are to grow.

During many conversations I discovered that, for some, coming to faith later in life was dramatic. One colleague spoke of finding themself on their knees in a hospital chapel while they awaited news of a very sick loved one. In my case, mercifully, it involved a simple and inexorable series of binary decisions to be made. These binary decisions did not come to resolution easily. My path to faith in Jesus Christ was a winding and recursive path. There were conversations with so many. Some conversations were explicitly about faith while others were about other business. All seemed ultimately to draw me back to the faith question. There were many times when I turned back. As my journey progressed, it was not a major leap for

7. Matt 7:13–14.

me to accept the existence of God as Creator of all things. Accepting Christ was a very major decision. It may be for you.

I think that there may be another reason why it is called the narrow gate: if we amass too many possessions and try to carry them through, we just won't fit. There is a call here to be generous with what we have been given.

Calling and Liminal Spaces

In *Strengthening the Soul of Your Leadership*, Ruth Haley Barton presents a view of one's soul that is stark in its simplicity. She says, "When I refer to the soul, I am not talking about some ill-defined, amorphous, soft-around-the-edges sort of thing. I am taking about the part of you that is most real—the very essence of you that God knew before he brought you forth in physical form, the part that will exist after your body goes into the ground."[8] I accept this perspective. Perhaps, then, it is our soul that fully hears God's word to us. I will come back to this.

The prophet Jeremiah said, "Now the word of the Lord came to me saying, 'Before I formed you in the womb, I knew you.'"[9] This was a comforting passage for me to find; giving me at once both the notion that God not only formed our spiritual as well as physical being, but he anticipates our actions and is at work in our lives, encouraging us, patiently forgiving our many shortcomings, and celebrating our journey toward him. If we are this important to God, then I would venture further to say that we are reflections *of* God (cf. Gen 1: 26).

Returning to Moses, in the book of Numbers we find a description of this leader of Israel, "Now the man Moses was very humble, more so than anyone else on the face of the earth."[10] Moses is the archetype—the role model for a leader who took the hard

8. Barton, *Strengthening the Soul of Your Leadership*, 13.

9. Jer 1:5.

10. Num 12:3.

road rather than the easy road. His call to task was to lead his people to the promised land, yet he personally, in the end, did not enter, as we learn in Deuteronomy. We should have a deep understanding of the purpose of our endeavours; the why and not simply the what of our undertakings.

Remembering the why requires time for reflection. So many speak of the need for solitude and quietness; perhaps this is when our souls do the most listening. I have learned that this is a key discipline for all those who seek after God. In my experience, moving into solitude can be challenging, even daunting. In an article published in the journal *Practical Theology*, I wrote this:

> Genesis 32 tells the story of Jacob, who, having sent his family and entourage across a stream, 'was left alone' (Gen. 32:24). In this alone-ness; Jacob's night of struggle depicts his personal struggle as prelude to exposure to the divine. I have encountered and counselled a number of mid-career men who are searching for faith.
>
> Through conversation we often discuss a fear of a potential first encounter with the divine, because we speak about silence as a form of alone-ness—no distractions, just silence—a time of personal, and sometimes fearful, introspection and, often for the first time, contemplation of prayer. The discussion of fearfulness arises because this is the moment, frequently, when our past sins and errors—all the miss-steps of the first decades of our lives—take on the proportions of Jacob's struggle as described in the Genesis passage. Beyond this, to choose silence in a life that is full of noise and action can be an alien thought. This fear can and does frequently prevent us from acquiescing to silence, effectively preventing the potential divine encounter that may follow. Thus, I suggest that there is a spiritual journey to be made here; a distinct progression from the void of silence, into a spiritual stillness and solitude turning to surrender and divine encounter. This progression is as follows:
>
> • Silence: An experience of loneliness, fear; possibly a struggle with past sins and errors. One may flee from silence.

- Solitude: A place of stillness and peace. An experience of openness to reflection and, perhaps, prayer.

- Willing surrender: A moment of divine encounter and spiritual transformation—becoming a new person in Christ.[11]

In his poem, *Ash Wednesday*, T. S. Eliot wrote, "teach us to sit still."[12] I think that Eliot is urging us to enter a liminal space, disquieting as it can be on occasion.

It is crucial that we find a way to let silence pierce through the noise of the day, without fear or apprehension. While we must seek strength and resilience, we must overcome the temptation to be powerful. It is setting aside time for daily reflection that enables this; perhaps assisted by prayer—prayer that focuses on thanksgiving and the sanctification of God's name. This discipline enables us to *pull ourselves back* from acts that might take us in the wrong path. Shrinking before God is a common demand in most world religions. The word *Islam* infers surrender and submission to God. In the Hebrew *Tanakh* we hear the words of an angel (some believe it was Gabriel) who spoke the following words to Daniel after Daniel threw himself prostrate on the ground in surrender, "Have no fear Daniel, for from the first day that you set your mind to get understanding, practicing abstinence before your God, your prayer has been heard."[13] Our prayers *are* heard.

As I began my own faith journey I began to pray. It was awkward and very clumsy at the beginning, and I'm still not sure if I really understand how to do this. Once again, I found that the Sermon on the Mount in the Gospel of Matthew provides Jesus' own instruction on prayer. He said, "But when you pray, go into your room and shut the door and pray to your Father who is in secret; and your Father who is in secret will reward you."[14] The reward is, I think, that when you are alone, still and small, God will work on quieting your soul; bringing strength and restoration. If you need evidence that this is taking

---

11. Bates, "Paracletic Ministry," 66.

12. Eliot, *Waste Land*, 53.

13. Dan 10:12.

14. Matt 6:6.

place, you will begin to notice that your interactions with others, especially in difficult situations, will be different. There will be less bombast in your response, you will be calmer, and you will be more empathetic. Those close to you will notice this change in you—perhaps even before you do. This was certainly the case for me. Jonathan Pennington points out the importance that Jesus places on the issue of, "The heart/inner person and internal/external righteousness."[15] It is in quiet prayer away from others that we reach for this divine encounter—reaching for uprightness. We do not always find it.

I have come to realize that accepting faith in Jesus does not mean that the skies suddenly brighten and everything becomes clear sailing. On the contrary, it can actually mean that life becomes considerably more challenging. This has certainly been my own experience. Perhaps it is the increased depth of engagement that causes us to encounter new demands and complications; yet we seem able to cope. The message of the Jesus story is, as Henri Nouwen describes, "the suffering, death, burial and resurrection of Jesus . . . God's love, which Jesus wants us to see, is shown to us by his becoming a partner and a companion in our suffering, thus enabling us to turn it into a way to liberation."[16] This is a big issue, perhaps one part of the mystery of God that is hardest to grasp: Surrender leads to liberation.

Self-Restraint

When Jesus says "Blessed are the poor in spirit," (Matt 5:3) I don't think we are required to be meek in the spineless sense, but rather in the patient and mild sense. I have said from time to time, "Don't confuse kindness with softness." We can still make the difficult decisions, but they will be made with greater care. I invite you to dwell also on the sixth Beatitude, "Blessed (happy) are the pure in heart, for they will see God" (Matt 5:8). We must constantly pull ourselves

15. Pennington, *Sermon on the Mount and Human Flourishing,* 210.

16. Nouwen, *Letters to Marc about Jesus,* 30.

away from behavior that puts impurities back into our hearts. Jesus is saying, effectively, that we will find happiness in self-restraint.

Awesome Things

Psalm 1 reads:

> Happy is the man who has not followed the counsel of the wicked, or taken the path of sinners, or joined the company of the insolent; rather, the teaching of the LORD is his delight, and he studies that teaching day and night. He is like a tree planted beside streams of water, which yields its fruit in season, whose foliage never fades, and whatever it produces thrives. Not so the wicked; rather, they are like chaff that wind blows away. Therefore, the wicked will not survive judgment, nor will sinners, in the assembly of the righteous. For the LORD cherishes the way of the righteous, but the way of the wicked is doomed.[17]

A little while ago a restaurant server described their daily sandwich to me as awesome! Such gastronomic delights certainly can be good, even really good, but hardly awe-inspiring. Here's something that truly is awesome, even *epic*: The word *eschaton* comes to us from the Ancient Greek word meaning "end." Literally, it is the last thing, the *end of this current time*, the climax of history. There are many views on exactly what this means—we need to think about this and come to our own decision about it. The last chapters of The Revelation to John describe the climax of the *eschaton*. We read that, "Also, another book was opened, the book of life. And the dead were judged according to their works, as recorded in the books."[18] As we read on to Revelation 21:1 and John's vision of "a new heaven and a new earth," we are led to the question of whether there is an enduring value of our work at the end of days; at the *eschaton*. To answer this question, we must also come to a conclusion as to whether the

---

17. Ps 1:1–6, *TANAKH.*
18. Rev 20:12b.

new creation is achieved through *Annihilato Mundi*, the complete destruction of our current creation, or through *Transformatio Mundi*, the transformation of the world. I personally accept the *Transformatio Mundi* view. Donald Gowan writes:

> The [Hebrew Scripture] vision of the future deals throughout with the world in which we now live. All was made by God, so nothing is bad in itself, but sin has by now left it hopelessly corrupted . . . To the challenge that has been raised concerning the appropriateness of calling the [Hebrew Scripture] hope 'eschatology,' asking 'end of what?' it will be shown (in Gowan's book) that a clear answer can be given. The answer is: 'the end of evil.'[19]

While Ezekiel confirms God will make things right, Jesus asserts that there will be judgment. In the closing verses of Jesus' Sermon on the Mount, we read:

> Not everyone who says to me, 'Lord, Lord,' will enter the kingdom of heaven, but only he who does the will of my Father who is in heaven. Many will say to me on that day, 'Lord, Lord, did we not prophesy in your name, and in your name drive out demons and perform many miracles?' Then I will tell them plainly, 'I never knew you. Away from me, you evildoers!'[20]

Pennington writes, "It is appropriate that Jesus gives these warnings at the end of the sermon—because all of the discourse is framed in the context of eschatological urgency."[21] With this theological foundation in view, I draw a deep, spiritual purpose in our working lives. This spiritual purpose is God's summons to us to dedicate our vocations to service to the kingdom—more than personal wealth accumulation and self-aggrandizement—both now and in preparation for the new creation. In other words, our work is our *legacy*—our *intentional* commitment. This spiritual orientation is the grounding for a critical understanding of a lifetime of work

---

19. Gowan, *Eschatology in the Old Testament*, 2.

20. Matt 7: 21–23.

21. Pennington, *Sermon on the Mount and Human Flourishing*, 271.

wherein we will strive unceasingly to reflect the image of Christ in our methods and in our demeanor in the workplace.

The creation account in Genesis is a narrative of purpose for humankind. God "breathed into his nostrils the breath of life" (Gen 2:7). Indeed, we are formed of his essence and we are created to provide custodianship of his creation. There is no doubt that after the fall our tasks take on greater exertion (cf. Gen 3:14). We are, however, equipped for it.

Psalm 92 is a song for the Sabbath day and begins, "It is good to give thanks to the Lord." As Genesis 1:15 makes clear, man was made to till the garden. It was the fall that introduced the *burden* of work. This opens us to the reality that the intent of work has not changed; work has, and always had, divine purpose. This brings to mind the notion that fallen mankind might find redemption in work, if that work is noble. Stefan Wyszynski states this in the form of an apparent paradox when he says, "Work, by its difficulty, redeems, ennobles, and sanctifies."[22] Exodus makes it clear that we are to rest from our labor if we are to fulfill our efforts in a way that is holy, "Six days you shall labor and do all your work. But the seventh day is a Sabbath day to the Lord your God."[23] This tells us that we need a rhythm in our lives. We need to restore in our lives the cycle of work-rest-play-worship-work. Without this rhythm we risk major breakdown and loss of purpose.

Our daily work, in all its domains and forms, is a critical and beloved contribution to God's kingdom, both in the now, as broken as the now is, and the not yet. Indeed, the significance of our work, as our means to respond to God's vocational call to us, is eschatological in its importance. We have work to do in the service of God and his kingdom; work that is more important than we might imagine.

22. Wyszynski, *All You Who Labor*, 82.
23. Exod 20:10.

Gandalf & Frodo

Many of us have read the *Lord of the Rings* trilogy by J. R. R. Tolkien, or we have watched the movie adaptation. In *The Fellowship of the Ring*, we witness an exchange between Gandalf and Frodo. Frodo states, "I wish it had not happened in my time." Gandalf replies, "So do I and so do all who live to see such times. But that is not for them to decide. All we have to do is decide what to do with the time that is given us."[24] The imagery of this dialogue between the hobbit Frodo and his guiding wizard Gandalf is such that it calls to mind, in all of us, a time when we are presented with a pivotal decision: to step up or to step down, to take the easy or wide road, or, in response to our Lord's instruction, to enter through the narrow gate.

There is a narrow gate out there for us all. It cannot be missed; and we will have to choose.

What if the Future Could Be as Clear as the Past?

One of the enjoyable pastimes of my life was competitive sailing. Sometimes I single-handed, but often it was around the buoys—after work on Wednesday summer evenings with co-workers. We generally had a crew of five or six. Each had a specific job to do. Generally, I was the foredeck guy, which meant that my task was mainly to wrestle with the spinnaker. This included getting the spinnaker flying properly, then getting it down, taking it below decks (where it was always hot), and stuffing it carefully in its bag, ready to fly again, and to get it back on the foredeck for the next downwind spinnaker run. Plus, because I was usually physically the smallest member of the crew, I was also tasked with being hoisted to the top of the mast to clear line jams. There is nothing like swinging through a sixty-degree arc in choppy water while clearing a jam,

24. Tolkien, *Fellowship of the Ring*, 67.

being yelled at from below, clinging to the mast and offering, I'll admit, a few colorful words to those down on deck who were kindly offering me instructions.

Our skipper always had a plan that was different from every other in the race. As we crossed the start line, he would always veer off in a direction generally perpendicular to the rest of the fleet. Occasionally this seemed to bode well for us, but more often we ended up crossing the finish line when everyone else was already tied up back at the dock and telling stories to one another! Could we have seen the outcome from the beginning? I'll never know.

In a different role, however, I learned something interesting. As a securities regulator, sitting on adjudicative panels, I found, with a fairly high degree of accuracy, that I could work my way backwards through the events and financial transactions given in evidence, to arrive at the moment when the wrong path was taken—and my task then was to determine the cause for the path taken from that point forward, thus leading to the issue that had brought the respondent in front of the regulatory tribunal. Had this been a deliberate act? Had it been a really bad and unfortunate error? Why hadn't someone in the organization played out in their minds the potential result of the path that was being chosen?

It's actually not that difficult. There's a reason why regulators speak of the guiding minds of an organization—these minds are there to guide! Guiding includes a discipline of standing, figuratively, some period of time beyond a critical decision before it is made. Yet we see, time after time, the evidence that this really important work has not been done. The strategic imperative gives way to the expedient: it always ends badly.

Sometimes an alarm is triggered by someone further down in the organization, but they don't speak up for whatever reason, usually fear. Perhaps they do speak up and are ignored.

This is why we have to be willing to embrace contrary perspectives around the table when key decisions are being contemplated. Oddly, we often describe those that have a laser-like vision on a future unseen by others as brilliant. We can all name several such individuals. I offer that this is a learned brilliance—often which comes from seeking counsel.

Perhaps a term to anchor this process is *legacy*. I invite you, today, to take time to pull out a piece of paper and write down what a decision today is starting to look like when contemplated in legacy terms. Looked at this way we ask, "Can we still live with it?"

Eschatology and Work

Thinking about *eschatology* does not mean that we allow our days to be consumed by fretting about the end of time. Indeed, in the Sermon on the Mount, Jesus asserts, "So do not worry about tomorrow, for tomorrow will bring enough troubles of its own. Today's trouble is enough for today."[25]

My father had a saying, "Today is the tomorrow that you worried about yesterday." The word "time" appears 771 times in the Bible. *Webster's New College Dictionary* describes time as, "every moment that has ever been or ever will be."[26] Time culminates in the *end of days* of which the angel spoke to Daniel (cf. Dan 10:14). My studies are involved with not only precepts of faith for the here and now, but also with what we do with our days in preparation for, and as contribution to, time's *other*: eternity.

Deep happiness today, I would offer, is linked to our expectation of eschatological happiness. While this argument is profoundly appealing, there is no question that it is difficult to grasp in the absence of faith. This is particularly challenging in a culture where the prevailing approach is "life is hard and then you die," so take whatever you can take in the here and now. Sadly, this view seems to be undergirding a growing model of living, exemplified frequently by some leaders who seem to escalate from one level of obfuscation to another—wrapping themselves in professed biblical aphorisms.

There is, I would offer, a reassuring answer to these troubling questions. Notwithstanding the pressure to normalize with the prevailing worldly view, sooner or later, a great number of us seek to

---

25. Matt 6:34.
26. *Webster's New World College Dictionary*, 1499.

answer the questions: "How might we know what to do with the days that have been given us?," "May we find sanctification in our work?," "In what way will we be held to account for that work?," and "What will be our legacy?" Often struggling with such questions alone, many, if not most, find these questions daunting. If you do not belong to a faith community, or have family, friends, or other trusted advisors with whom you can enter into dialogue with, you may wish to seek someone out. From research conducted in my doctoral work, it appears that, sadly, very few find, or even seek, such conversations.

As alluded to elsewhere, in a profound apocalyptic vision, the angel that many scholars identify as Gabriel spoke to Daniel and said that he had "come to help you [Daniel] understand what will happen to your people at the end of days."[27] This statement is fundamentally apocalyptic—an *unveiling of*—the absolute end of the age; when the book of life will be opened. This responds to our need to seek answers to the questions that we wrestle with very much in the present. Daniel draws us deeply into this contemplation. If the *eschaton* is the nexus between time and eternity, then every event carries an eschatological meaning. Arguably, this places our everyday work, together with the ethics with which we carry out that work, squarely within the gravitas of such perspective. This eschatological perspective—transformation—clarifies the relationship between human beings, their efforts, and creation; worthy of contemplation, indeed. This calls for time to find a quiet spot.

The apostle Paul appears to support the view that work is a response to God's call. In his letter to the Colossians, Paul states, "Whatever your task, put yourselves into it, as done for the Lord and not for your masters, since you know that from the Lord you will receive your inheritance as your reward; you serve the Lord Christ."[28] I suggest that this inheritance is peace in the knowledge that you have carried out what you were called upon to do. It is that simple, and yet so very significant.

27. Dan 10:14.
28. Rom 8:22–23.

The words of the gospel hymn, "The Mistakes of My Life,"[29] will resonate with all who are called to faith in adulthood—the hymn begins with the words, "The mistakes of my life have been many, the sins of my heart have been more." The good news is that through faith we are justified, set straight again and, through baptism, given new strength. Our work, done right, becomes sacramental. It is my belief that we are *sealed* as worthy of God's kingdom by the example that we set in the carrying out of our labors, by the power of the Holy Spirit. Indeed, elemental to this is that, for most people, sanctification takes place in the daily routine of their work. A respondent to a research questionnaire wrote, "I know that all work, regardless of its value on Earth, should be done with the same passion as if working for Jesus directly."[30] It is the gradual process of a lifetime of work in which we are to strive unceasingly to reflect the image of Christ and to seek personal sanctification. In other words, our task is the constant pursuit of holiness to the greatest extent we can achieve in this life, plus a hoped-for divine acknowledgment of our demonstration of accountability to him in the stewardship of our gifts for the enrichment of his kingdom.

Turning Points

Inflection can be described as a turning: a bend, or a curve. In business, and in personal life, this term is used to describe a time of impending significant change. Turning points come in many forms; some chosen, many imposed.

Turning points can occur in the form of reversing course when we realize we are on the wrong path and need to get back to the place where the decision was made so that we can choose a right path. Pausing for discernment is crucial.

I firmly believe that our lifetime of work is desired by God as a contribution to unfolding history: indeed, each of us can make a

---

29. Composer: Robert Lowry.
30. Respondent to my doctoral research questionnaire.

personal difference—each of us *will* make a personal difference; for good or for bad. Also, following our conversion and the acceptance of faith in Jesus Christ, our work becomes the gradual path toward personal sanctification—to be set straight, purified, and made holy—guided by the in-working of the Holy Spirit in each of us as we navigate the way. We become authentic, complete persons.

Long-distance running, horse-riding, and sailing, for me, involved numerous little failures, both physical and psychological. These experiences, in addition to work experiences and challenges, resulted in my becoming more complete. These were all part of a deepening of my sense of personhood and my destiny.

Don't fret when a turning point occurs. There is new growth ahead; possibly a complete transformation.

Take a Little Off the Top

I haven't told many about this—until now! A significant series of new learnings and experiences occurred for me when I transitioned from the private sector to the public sector. After a lengthy series of fairly intensive interviews, I learned that I would be appointed to a new role. The person to whom I would report invited me to breakfast to discuss the details of the appointment. One of the items to be raised would be my compensation. My soon-to-be new superior affirmed what I already knew—advising me that the role would not meet the compensation level that I would have received in the private sector. Wait, what? No, seriously, I replied that, before being advised of my new salary, I would accept it, and in fact commit to giving ten percent of it back to the institution as a charitable donation, which I did for the rest of my contract. I had remembered someone once saying, "Are you concerned about the ten percent you're giving up or the ninety percent that you're keeping?" The truth is that I did not miss the compensation given back. Now to be fair, this may not be the circumstance that everyone experiences or can afford. We all give back in different ways as we are called.

What My Horse Taught Me about Leadership

Are you safe to be with? Are you fit to be a leader? It was a long time ago now that I first started to ride, and eventually to own, a horse. Somewhere along the way I found Tom Widdicombe's book, *Be with Your Horse*. I recall Widdicombe explaining that every horse has two questions: "Am I safe with you?" and "Are you fit to be my leader?"[31]

My first horse, Mark, had a habit of heading off to the farthest spot in the paddock whenever he saw me coming to get a lead rope on him. Then when I got close to him, he would bolt to another distant spot. One day, I stood in the paddock, and once I knew that he had seen me, I simply turned my back to him, and waited. It took a while, but eventually, after some meandering, he walked up behind me and rested his head on my shoulder. Trust was established. I also have to admit that it brought a few tears to my eyes.

I realized that my equine relational experiences actually had value in the workplace. Our staff, too, essentially have safety-related questions. They ask, "What's expected of me?" and "How am I doing?" These questions require answers.

Are you safe to be with? Are you fit to be a leader? Will you serve those that seek to serve the organization, and to flourish in the process? As leaders we are the custodians of the company's ethics and values. Right and wrong are truly powerful concepts. They are borne aloft in the culture that we permit and uphold.

And who knows, maybe you'll enjoy the ride!

Solitude and Community

I am now involved in ministry as an ordained deacon in the Anglican Church of Canada. Although I spend time in community, the truth is, however, that I am a bit of a loner. I always preferred sports where I could compete as an individual rather than as a team member. I

---

31. Widdicombe, *Be with Your Horse*, 17.

did play rugby, but I was a winger, and you're on your own on the wing—well, until you get tackled! I preferred track and field. Later in life I took up distance running, sailing, and horseback riding—all essentially individual activities. In my view there is little that brings a greater opportunity for reflection that the solitude of physical competition alone. I kept my own company and I was seldom lonely when alone. I calculate that I have run the equivalent of the circumference of the planet, although it has been some years since I pulled such distance runs. I remember that I eschewed the temptation to listen to music, choosing instead to simply allow the world around me and heaven above to soak in. I have to admit that one marathon was a challenge of loneliness. The Detroit Marathon, when I participated in it, was a day of horizontal driving rain, and a good portion of the course was on Belle Island in the Detroit River (you might be familiar with it). There were few spectators, and I was cold, wet, and tired. However, I discovered something interesting: when I looked down at the road too long, I would come to a stop, exhausted, but when I looked up at the sky and toward the horizon, I could keep going.

I have found strong personal direction in my own journey— one from finding faith alone, eventually to realizing the need to connect with others. Slowly a balance emerged. On the one hand, I reflected on the number of times that we read of Jesus' withdrawal from his disciples and from the crowd to be alone in prayer and reflection. I contemplate Jesus' own words in the Sermon on the Mount, "And whenever you pray, do not be like the hypocrites; for they love to stand and pray in the Synagogues and the street corners, so that they may be seen by others. Truly I tell you, they have received their reward."[32] Indeed, we must pray in private. However, on the other hand, I have also witnessed the power of communal prayer. I think that Jesus' point was to admonish us to pray with humility, with our focus on God, not on who might be watching us.

I have learned both through my studies and through dialogue that a Christian life is experienced both in private prayer and in serving community; indeed, there can be no proportionality to our offer of help to others. In her book, *Caring*, author Nel Noddings

32. Matt 6:5–6.

speaks of the obligation of engrossment in the lives of those we are committed to care for. This is serious business. Mentoring others, caring for those we agree to mentor, means that we must engross ourselves in their situation. We can't do this from a safe distance. Nowhere have I experienced this more than with interaction over the decades with university students at four campuses. Mentorship is hugely important for the student mentee, but it is equally rewarding to the mentor.

A *large* mentorship opportunity, in my view, is the critical need to engage in a dialogue of discovery of diversity, understanding, and respect for people of all backgrounds and faiths. Cedric Herring writes, "Diversity is associated with increased sales revenue, more customers, greater market share, and greater relative profits."[33]

There are lessons here. The deliberate and focused act of seeking racial and gender diversity in our work and community environments will strengthen those environments deeply.

The Journey to Faith

My faith journey was a slow burn. For the longest time I kept my return to faith to myself. This ended when the front cover of the November 2001 issue of *Toronto Life Magazine* heralded the story, "Born Again on Bay Street: Patricia Best on Why the Suits are Turning to God."[34] This story followed an interview that I gave to journalist and writer Patricia Best, in which we discussed my coming to faith, and the ways in which this development in my life was impacting my career, my perspectives on leadership and client service interaction, and my conversations with colleagues. This was a pivotal moment. My faith decision was no longer a secret. Some were surprised, some felt that I had gone soft in the head, and was no longer capable of leadership, of making the tough decisions.

33. Herring, "Does Diversity Pay?," 219.
34. Best, "Born Again on Bay Street."

Many, though, were not at all surprised. Best of all, however, was the many conversations that followed.

Coming to faith changed me, and changed the way I see others.

Sometimes Correction Is Required

Leaders are struggling perhaps as never before. As I write this, I have just read of the terrible and disastrous decision by a mining company to destroy an ancient aboriginal cave system in Australia. Organizations risk becoming twisted and broken. Second Peter 3:3–4 offers, "First of all you must understand this, that in the last days scoffers will come, scoffing and indulging their own lusts and saying, 'where is the promise of his coming?'" Perhaps a significant challenge is that we have come to define ourselves only by what we do, rather than why we do what we do. It may be time for us to be as vocal about the purpose of our work as well as the details of our work. We must remember that a spirit-filled life is one where we are constantly conscious of the need to model behavior that is focused on those placed in our care, at home, at work, in the classroom, and in mentorship.

Ethics, Culture, and Long-Term Performance

While short-term performance can be forced, I want to offer that long-term performance is tied, inextricably, to ethics and culture. So, what can we do to build a business that flourishes, that is valued, and that endures?

Perhaps the place to begin is to contemplate how deeply we should adhere to the maxim that the values that we model are the values that are embraced by those who work with us. People listen to what we say in the boardroom or the classroom, and then they watch how we behave in the hallways. If our behavior is inconsistent, others are confused at best, or they write us off completely and follow their own path.

Let me offer that every one of us has an opportunity to build a nation—the *triple bottom line* is how we build a nation: we make a decent profit, we engage in the development of our community, and we consider how we can provide work for others that not only gives them an appropriate wage and benefits, but allows them dignity and the opportunity to fulfill their potential.

And guess what? We will be remembered for our work, long after we have finished working. This is legacy.

Hospitality and Commerce

The beginning of commerce in the ancient world provides us with a critical clue for the essence of enduring leadership. Imagine yourself as a traveling merchant on a dusty village road in the ancient world around dusk. There is not a motel in sight, and no street lamps either. It's going to be dark soon, and you are getting anxious. You knock on a door. The homeowner takes you in, offers you a bowl of water to clean up, then a meal, then a safe place to sleep. You talk about your business. In the morning you offer a small payment or a gift, perhaps even the offer of a little work before you leave; then you continue on your way, probably with a few leads as to who to call on, perhaps with a reputation that is just a little better than yesterday. Thus, hospitality and commerce are combined. Indeed, without hospitality your very life in commerce may not have lasted very long.

Meanness and Generosity

Are you mean or generous? And seriously, do you really see life as a zero-sum game?[35]

35. If someone else wins, it must be at your expense.

Paul K. Bates

Kindness does not equate to weakness. You can be every bit the strong and effective leader and still leave others feeling satisfied and heard. Justice, decisiveness, measuredness, generosity, and care can all be combined with strong and effective leadership.

Biblical Leaders

Scripture is replete with stories of leadership. In Ezra-Nehemiah, we find stories of two leaders who understood the need for centred and spirit-filled leadership. First is the story of Cyrus, the king of Persia, a leader whose management style still resonates today. Recognizing the need for healing and inclusiveness in a changed environment, Cyrus declared, "The LORD, the God of heaven, has given me all the kingdoms of the earth and he has charged me to build him a house at Jerusalem in Judah. Any of those among you who are of his people—may their God be with them!—are now permitted to go up to Jerusalem in Judah and rebuild the house of the LORD, the God of Israel."[36]

Second is the story of Nehemiah, who, guided by divine inspiration, responded to King Cyrus's offer. Nehemiah returned to Judah and, despite considerable opposition from among his own people in Jerusalem, led the rebuilding of the wall, giving all the glory to God, "I told them that the hand of my God had been gracious upon me."[37] Times of upheaval present a great need for strong, restorative leadership, often at significant personal risk. Indeed, Nehemiah learned that just because one steps up to offer leadership, does not necessarily mean many wish to follow.

36. Ezra 1:2b–3b.
37. Neh 2:18.

Hubris Can Cause Blindness

I reflect on a June 2010 headline story as recorded by the Reuters news service, which read, "BP CEO Tony Hayward, on the front lines of his company's battle to contain the massive Gulf of Mexico oil spill, apologized . . . for saying he wants his 'life back.'" Thankfully, his personal reflection drew Hayward to recognize that, with his leadership role, he had forfeited the right to put his own interests first, and he offered an apology.[38] Conquering personal hubris is a critical step to effective leadership. Hubris is described as wanton insolence or arrogance resulting from excessive pride.[39] In my experience, hubris becomes akin to an addiction—it may be among the worst of all addictions.

Hubris can cause a blindness to issues that are right in front of us. We must make a habit of visiting the hallways, shop floors, loading docks, wards, and offices. People need to be liberated by giving ear to them. It is more than listening to the conversation; it is being *present*. As Maya Angelou is reported to have said, "I've learned that people will forget what you said, people will forget what you did, but people will never forget how you made them feel."[40]

Management by Walking Around

Yes, management by walking around is important. A colleague once told me an interesting story. She had a middle-level field sales manager who resigned to take on a role with another firm. Curious, she decided not to replace him for about six months. Here's what happened—nothing! There was no change in the sales performance of the team that had reported to this individual and no change in anything else, for example client loss or expense control.

38. "BP CEO Apologizes," para. 1.

39. *Merriam-Webster*, s.v. "hubris (n.)," https://www.merriam-webster.com/dictionary/hubris.

40. https://www.goodreads.com/author/quotes/3503.Maya_Angelou.

On enquiry, she discovered that members of the individual's team could not recall the last time they had received a visit from, made a joint sales call with, held a meeting with, or had any other direct, personal, interaction with their manager. This vignette reminds me of the critical need to make management by walking around a critical part of our leadership routine. Here's why.

First and foremost is the need to model leadership behavior. You might just be amazed how powerful it can be to simply be the kind of employee that you desire everyone else in your organization to be. They will watch you intently! They will listen to your words, your tone, your responses to questions, and they will watch your body language—even without realizing it. This enables you to carry your organization's lexicon to every person in the organization, and this will translate into the way folks not only treat one another, but how they respond to customers as well. Of course, these brief conversations also enable you to recognize and respond more immediately to instances of ineffectiveness, or gaps in knowledge and approach, thus giving rise to the opportunity to be a curbside coach, giving meaningful guidance right in the thick of day-to-day activity.

Vision and Loneliness

Authentic leaders experience loneliness—I would venture that occasionally this can be profound loneliness. *In loneliness, we can lose, and yet gain, our vision.* The gifts of vision and reasoning are separate and distinct gifts. Some possess both, others none, still others one or the other. If one is to believe in, and ultimately perceive the details of, the big idea, one is going to be alone from time to time in order for these gifts to be employed. The apostle Paul understood the challenge of laying out a vision. He was the *contextualizer* for a reason—he knew that each audience had to receive the vision in language and imagery which aligned with their own familiar surroundings and cultural awareness. We see this in the Epistle to the Romans especially. De Silva asserts that in Romans, "Paul provides his fullest treatment of the way God has brought together people of diverse heritage and practice into one body of the church, and he also gives several chapters of practical advice for preserving unity in the midst of this diversity."[41] Consider, for example, Romans 7, where Paul confesses, in detail, his own struggle with sin. For those of us that miss the mark from time to time this is valuable. Paul's conversion involved deep loneliness, resulting in new vision.

Never Accelerate into a Closing Gap

My father taught me to drive in a 1950s-era car. It had a steering column-mounted three-speed shifter, and a very stiff clutch! But it was the promise of freedom on the open road and I could not wait to test its upper limits, if you know what I mean! Sensing my enthusiasm, one of the mantras my father drilled into me was, "*Never accelerate into a closing gap.*" Indeed, remembering this advice— sometimes at the last moment—saved me from some hair-raising moments, or worse.

As the years passed and my career unfolded, I came to learn that this mantra had a figurative as well as a literal application. Here's the reality: trying to cover an error with what turns out to be another error will always end in disaster. Indeed, to stay with the automotive theme, we can all name at least one major iconic brand whose senior leadership may be ruminating over this truth right now.

How to Cut through the Fog of Today

In an editorial that I wrote for the Conference Board of Canada some years ago, I offered that, "The fog of current circumstances can be cut through only if you can stand in the future and describe that future in a level of detail that is as specific as your organization's

---

41. deSilva, *Introduction to the New Testament*, 598.

current circumstances."[42] Sometimes the clarity you need can only be achieved by bringing trusted and impartial advisors into the dialogue. While this is a critical discipline when contemplating strategic decisions, it also has importance in everyday business. Culture establishes the rules that we manage by. During my days on the trading desk, when an error occurred, like trying to close a short position by selling—only to end up with twice the original short position, we had a hard rule—flatten the trade and take the loss—never try to trade it out. Take the loss and move on.

Dealing decisively and transparently with missteps can be costly, but never as costly as the impending financial or reputational hit that lurks when the first error is not dealt with head-on.

When short-termism takes precedence in decision-making, the long-term invariably is mortgaged, if not sacrificed completely. Stakeholders and regulators will generally be lenient on errors, but they will not forgive cover-ups.

Mysticism

In its most straightforward interpretation, *mysticism* is the doctrine that offers a belief that it is possible to achieve communion with God through a discipline of contemplation, or meditation. Why does this appear to be so hard? Why doesn't God just slap us in the face and say, "LOOK!" This is the hard part of free choice that God has *chosen* to give to us. This search is more difficult for us today than ever as we are constantly bombarded by those that do choose to get in our face. Contemplation offers a way for us to reflect on God's invitation to us. I have to say that it also opens us up to vulnerability, and possibly to attack. In Romans 7:21, Paul says, "So I find it to be a law that when I want to do good—evil lies close at hand." In other words, it is in ourselves. Jeff De Waal Dryden writes, "Paul discloses the psychological battles of a discordant self—ravaged by sin but at the same

---

42. Bates, "Corporation with Integrity," 2.

time testifying to signs of a new self, united in Christ."[43] In all the communities that Paul visited, he had a message that dark spiritual forces would be working on our psyche with the goal of turning us away from the call of faith. Are we tempted? Imagine that one is walking down a deserted street, an expensive car is parked with an open window and there is a beautiful coat on the seat; within easy reach. Well, maybe we do not even think about it, but . . .

Markets Are Built on Walls of Worry

To call volatile market dynamics jarring can be an understatement. Wild swings in the market not only put us on edge, but for some they put their entire portfolio strategy into question.

Do we bale out while the baling is good? Do we remember the maxim, "Buy into weakness?" Where do we turn to find the portfolio models that can help us determine a path forward? It would be easy to say that we have, "been through this before." Since entering the markets a half century ago, I have certainly been through extreme market turbulence. The truth, though, is that no situation can be cited to be a reflection or repeat of a previous situation. Every significant shock to the market is driven by its own unique set of events—the outcome, however, is always the same—prices will fall until they stop falling. For what it is worth, here are a few things to keep in front of us:

Changes in our perceptions of what is going on cause us all to reevaluate. The more risky or potentially long-term-wealth-destroying our perception becomes, the more likely our decision to make a precipitous change. A detailed assessment of the situation is critical to determining the specific change required. The resulting change is more likely to be received as appropriate.

The second is to remember, as is always the case, to look at the leadership of the businesses that your portfolios are comprised of. Capable hands on the tiller will usually steer the enterprise through

43. Dryden, "Revisiting Romans 7," 129.

challenging times. Market multiples will land where they will land. Experienced and capable leadership may be in shorter supply than one sometimes believes—especially in buoyant times. Look for the evidence of ethical and capable leadership and make your decisions and recommendations accordingly.

Finally think about your worst-case risk models, the ones that map probabilities of occurrence and severity of impact. In other words: How much downside risk can you take? If it looks like the potential decline is more significant than you can handle reasonably, it may be time to get out and reconsider.

Hope and the Prospect of Eternity

While *optimism* might be interpreted as cheerfully anticipating the best outcome in a challenging situation—the *optimum* result, to have true *hope,* is much more profound. Indeed, a hoped-for situation is one that we hold so deeply that we might actually rely on it. Paul's messages in Ephesus point to the state of our earthly lives within the context of the very significant new era being ushered in by the arrival of Jesus.

There were some communities in the early centuries following the life of Jesus that were of the view that they should stop working altogether and simply wait for Christ's return—the *parousia*. Our perspectives have evolved: Today we live in the "already, but not yet" frame of belief, called upon to conduct our lives as if the new kingdom is here, yet still to come. This is where hope and action meet, leading to victory.

Lectio Divina

We are invited to call on the Holy Spirit to enter our lives at all times, including at work. Recapturing the ancient practice of *Lectio Divina*, or divine reading, may assist us in the process of contemplation. Thelma Hall writes, "Long ago, and for many centuries, Lectio proved its great capacity as an effective instrument of the Holy Spirit in prayer, but today it is a 'treasure hidden in a field' of obscurity."[44] Hall goes on to offer:

> *Contemplation* is variously described as a 'resting' in God, or a 'loving gaze' upon him, or a 'knowing beyond knowing, or a 'rapt attention' to God. All such attempts at verbalizing the experience fail to express the reality, for the simple reason that contemplation transcends the thinking and reasoning of meditation, as well as the emotions and 'feelings' of the affective faculties. It is basically a prayer and experience of pure faith.[45]

Bringing deep, daily reflection into our routine will bring wholeness to our work. I encourage you to consider this. It has been challenging for me, but I do try every day, consciously, to put time aside for faithful contemplation.

It is worth considering that God asks no more of us than to work with him. This bears repeating: *God asks no more of us than to work with him.* Put simply, this means *same work—different purpose.*

Are There Forces Acting against Us?

Early in my faith walk I found strong resonance with the book of Daniel, particularly Daniel 10. In Daniel 10:12, Daniel is visited by the angel that many believe is Gabriel, where it is written, "Do not fear, Daniel, for from the first time you set your mind to gain understanding and to humble yourself before your God, your words have been heard." For quite a long time I focused solely on this verse as it gave me comfort to believe that God had perceived my personal change of heart and my prayers, that I had, indeed, begun to gain understanding and, I believe, to humble myself.

---

44. Hall, *Too Deep for Words*, 7.

45. Hall, *Too Deep for Words*, 9 (emphasis original).

I focused later on the verse that came next, "But the Prince of Persia opposed me twenty-one days, so Michael, one of the chief princes, came to help me." This passage (Dan 10:13) began an intense curiosity for me regarding the possibility of angelic beings, good and evil, in the cosmos, and in what ways, if any, their activities might impact humanity broadly and me personally. You may wish to ponder this also.

Stop Focusing on the Money

During my days in the academy, I have had the extraordinary honor and good fortune to interact, at some level or another, with some 10,000 undergraduate and graduate commerce, accounting, communications, and theology students. Indeed, it is a rush when, while walking along a downtown street, a former student yells out to me to stop and share with me the story of their career so far. Indeed, these days I get emails and LinkedIn updates from former students who are now, literally, around the globe.

Every speaking engagement, every class, every conversation, was and is truly energizing. One particular group discussion always stands out in my mind. That conversation is one that happened almost every year with first-year undergraduate commerce students, where I shared with them my life in the capital markets industry. One of the points that I emphasize is that one can make a good living, but don't do it simply for the money. Invariably, at the end of my talk, at least one student would ask, "How much money can you make?"

I don't blame them for asking this question. For one thing, the income one makes is a mark of success in an industry where, at the end of every day, one knows whether one is on the right or wrong side of a transaction from a profit perspective. To say that the capital markets industry is competitive is an understatement. I have had the pleasure of getting to know some extraordinarily charitable people who make their living in this sector. This drive for income dominance sometimes can, sadly, lead to the worst kind of hubris.

But here is the secret to how to make more money than you ever imagined. Stop focusing on the money! Focus on your clients. In an industry where everyone is debating the issue of a duty of best interest, my advice is to reach as far above such a threshold as you can possibly imagine. Consider starting by ensuring symmetry of information and then move on to building your legacy reputation with every client interaction.

In my early life as a business executive, my lawyer taught me this lesson. It was the first significant piece of legal work I needed to have done. My lawyer did the work and sent me his invoice—a big invoice! I called him and said that I was having trouble with his fee. He walked me through it, but at the end he said, "Paul, pay me what you think the work was worth." He was my corporate counsel for the rest of my career and is a close friend today, some forty years later, and he made good money from our firm—all of it earned. There's one thing that always precedes making a good living—trust! Oh, and I paid his bill as presented. I never questioned another invoice.

By the way, it is never too early to be philanthropic—first with your time and then with your money as well as with your time. I recall speaking with one of our country's renowned industrialists and philanthropists, who said to me, "Paul, money is like manure! If you pile it up it just stinks, but if you spread it around it does some good." Not all learn this. I have worked with people who made a lot of money and spent a dollar more than they made—not one penny to a charitable cause. Find a charity that you believe in and support it. It will not only inspire you, but it will also lead you to networks and people that you might never have come to know; people like the industrialist/philanthropist that I came to have conversations with.

The "Wind" of God

Iranian poet Forugh Farrokhzad wrote, "The wind will carry us."[46] I do not know for certain if Farrokhzad was drawing from the

---

46. Farrokhzad, "Wind Will Carry Us," line 25.

concept of *Ruh,* considered to be the wind of God, but this is certainly where her writing brought me to. It is interesting how close this word and its interpretation is to the Hebrew *Ruach,* which, according to the *Tanakh,* is God's instrument in creation. Genesis 1, the first book of Moses—the Torah—says, "When God began to create heaven and earth—the earth being unformed and void, with darkness over the surface of the deep and a wind from God sweeping over the water." This action by what we as Christians view as God's Holy Spirit takes on epic proportion.

Often associated with wind, fire, and breath, Genesis presents *Ruach* as the active agent in the redemption of chaos, the animation of creation—indeed the source of life—and the facilitation of human flourishing. If creation is a redemptive event, then the Holy Spirit is the first actor. Genesis 2:7 reads, "Then the Lord formed man from the dust of the ground and breathed into his nostrils the breath of life; and man became a living being." Thus, the spirit of God is *immanent*; present in ourselves and indeed in all creation.

It can be said also that the Holy Spirit inspires and empowers, as we read in Judges 3:10a, "And the spirit of the Lord came upon him [Othniel], and he judged Israel." It is apparent from Scripture that all living beings receive their breath of life from the Spirit for as long as they live. The Spirit is an abiding presence.

I have come to accept the *immanence* that we experience through Christ, who, in his earthly ministry, was the bearer of the Spirit, as is made emphatically clear at Jesus' baptism.

This brings me to a critical point: When do we offer witness to our faith to others? There is a broad diversity of approach among Christians in terms of their approach to proselytizing. My own approach is to seek, carefully and respectfully and only when invited, opportunities to engage in a faith dialogue. Once invited, my goal is to encourage reflection and contemplation; I leave the rest to the Holy Spirit. It is clear also that for some, their conversion is both fast and epiphanic; for others, as it was for me, it is a slow, almost methodical process.

The Message of Pentecost for Christians

The day of Pentecost was the fiftieth day after Passover, at the time of *Shavu'ot*—the Hebrew festival of weeks. The period from Passover to *Shavu'ot* is, for Jews, a time of great redemptive anticipation. For Jews, a key required reading on the first day of Pentecost is Ezekiel 1:1–28, which begins, "I looked, and lo, a stormy wind came sweeping out of the north—a huge cloud and flashing fire." Christians perceive this prophecy to have been fulfilled in the words of Acts 2:1, where we read,

> When the day of Pentecost had come, they were all together in one place. And suddenly from heaven there came a sound like the rush of a violent wind, and it filled the entire house where they were sitting. Divided tongues, as of fire, appeared among them and rested on each of them. All of them were filled with the Holy Spirit and began to speak in other languages, as the Spirit gave them ability.

The *telos* of our Christian lives is to share the new world with Jesus Christ and it appears that it is the *immanence*; the presence of the Holy Spirit in our lives that is preparing us for this. Indeed, Volf and others suggest that all our gifts are from the Spirit. Whether those skills are of the stone mason, the professor, the software creator, the nurse, the warehouse worker, or the investment banker, they are, if divinely inspired, skills of eschatological importance.

Not only is the Spirit at work as God's agent in our personal salvation, he is at work empowering us to become co-workers in the salvation of all creation, in all our vocational callings.

Our ability to do this is given energy by the Holy Spirit. It appears also that the Holy Spirit is equally active not only in the lives of individual Christians but in the church as a whole. In John 17:13–19, we find Jesus' prayer for his disciples, in which he says, "They do not belong to the world, just as I do not belong to the world" (v. 16). Jesus' disciples are instructed to work in the world, even though they do not belong to the world. In the same passage, Jesus prays for the disciples' protection. I believe that we must also pray for protection as we do our work *in* the world while avoiding the temptation to become *of* the world.

John 17:13–19 may be the heart of our challenge as we attempt to live a life in Christ. I recall that at a men's retreat some years ago, the speaker said, "For many, we may be the closest thing to Jesus Christ that they will experience!" I remember how this shook me as I came to grips with the gravity of this statement, not only for me personally as an emerging Christian, but for all us who are attempting to follow the way. Nothing about our faith gets more personal than this.

Integrity

I recently gave a talk to a large cohort of accounting students as they were completing their studies and preparing to seek employment as professional accountants. The next day I received an email from another presenter, an industry professional. Among other things, he wrote, "There is a great lack of integrity in organizations today. There appears to be little incentive for organizations to reverse this trend. Organizations, and government departments, do not care about their personnel and citizens." This might be an overstatement, but if this is even partially true, it requires our response. At the least, we must be ready to not be complicit in such situations. Where we can, we must find ways to confront and correct such behavior. This brings to mind some advice my mother gave me a long time ago. She told me to be wary of the first person to befriend me when starting a new role. She has been right too many times, sadly. In Paul's Letter to the Ephesians, we read, "Let no-one deceive you with empty words."[47] There will be times when one who is seeking power will attempt to influence you in advance of your effort to become completely familiar with a new environment. Keep in mind also that *nothing* is confidential.

---

47. Eph 5:6.

How can we withstand the pressure to become of the world while we actively participate in the world? If we are to have any hope, it seems to me that in our daily prayer and reflection we must remember our hope of Jesus Christ's role of *paraclete*, a Christ who comes alongside, who engrosses himself in our lives, and who, through the workings of the Holy Spirit, strengthens us.

Business Equilibrium

There is a sweet spot to be aspired to in your business endeavor where you achieve perfect equilibrium between client satisfaction and an appropriate profit margin for your business. I use the concept of equilibrium deliberately. Many service providers get completely skewed by focusing in one direction or the other; giving up client satisfaction for the sake of profitability, or profitability for the sake of the client experience. This point, of course, brings a critically important decision. There are times, consciously, when we give up profitability for the sake of the client experience. Such times would include the early stages of business growth, when business volumes have not reached the level needed for our target for profitability, and those times when, perhaps in resolution of an error, a decision is made to provide recompense in some form.

What I am saying, fundamentally, is that the client experience always comes first, especially if you plan to be around for a while. I am also saying though, that it is critical to have a specific pre-tax margin in view objectively, and then to monitor every element of the revenue and cost structure of your business in order to achieve and maintain that margin. This commitment to the client experience, especially when they are still a prospective client, might seem obvious, but I can tell you that it is not always the case.

Many major firms create numerous micro-segments of their client base to get a sense of an equilibrium profit margin for each segment. They then consider the implications this calculation must have on setting client expectations and then delivering against those expectations.

Paul K. Bates

In my first year of responsibility leading a retail investment business, I analyzed how much we were spending (Advertising and Promotion expenses) to acquire a customer. I then analyzed how much net profit we were earning per client—on average it was taking eighteen months to earn back the A & P investment. So, if we lost a customer within eighteen months net, we lost money on that client after deducting the average acquisition cost. We then undertook several key steps. We began with reducing the acquisition cost through analyzing the most effective methods to attract and acquire a customer—eventually getting acquisition cost to an average that was substantially less than where we had started. We also discovered that an effective client retention strategy did two things—it kept usage high and we also were able to increase what we called "share of wallet," i.e., using a second or third service from us. I also read somewhere that if you can keep a customer for two years, you will keep them indefinitely. Over my years in business, this proved largely to be true. You have probably calculated already that the cost involved in acquiring a new client is a multiple of the cost of keeping an existing client. Retention should be a critical focus.

Two Signatures

Some decades ago, I worked in a management role in an environment that included employees who were members of a trade union. Although this was a first for me, my father had been a trade unionist and I had seen the world through his eyes. My career brought me to an organization which had recently experienced a work stoppage. The particular department that I joined had experienced, and was continuing to experience, a number of union member grievances. I requested a meeting with the union leadership, at which I essentially made a promise and a request. In effect, I promised to take all grievances seriously, but at the same time I made the request that only critical grievances be brought forward. The union leadership team considered my request and agreed. Some months had passed when the same union leaders called for a meeting in order to present two grievances to me. Upon reading the files I agreed with the union leaders that these were real and meaningful issues which I would address. For the rest of my time in that role there were no further union grievances, and I valued the meaningful and productive relationship I proceeded to have with the union.

There are two signatures on an employment contract. They indicate a quest for mutual advantage. I realized that if I could live up to the commitments above management's signature, the union members would likely live up to theirs. The lesson is simple: live up to the expectations set by your signature. Our signature is a physical manifestation of our character.

Going the Extra Mile

In the First Letter of Peter, we read, "Always be ready to make your defense to anyone who demands from you an accounting for the hope that is within you; yet do it with gentleness and with reverence."[48] As Jesus himself demands, "If anyone forces you to go one mile, go also the second mile."[49] Coming to faith does not remove life's hardships and sorrows. My father had a saying, "Into every life a little rain must fall." Why is this? Why does it seem to me as if life has become even more challenging in the years since I accepted faith? Perhaps we are, like athletes, being tested and honed. In the Letter of James we read, "My brothers and Sisters, whenever you face trials of any kind, consider it nothing but joy, because you know that the testing of your faith produces endurance."[50]

48. 1 Pet 3:15.
49. Matt 5:41.
50. Jam 1:2–4.

Paul K. Bates

Alone but Never Deserted

During the Second World War, my father served in North Africa, among other campaigns. He never talked a lot about his war years, and so I was unaware until many years later, when I sorted through his belongings, that he had carried a medallion of St. Anthony of the Desert with him throughout his time in service.

All these years later, my faith journey has brought me to examine the life of St. Anthony of the Desert; an opportunity to learn why this desert father inspired my father so many years ago.

St. Anthony taught us that to be alone without being lonely is a critical gift. Perhaps I learned this most during my days of considerable long-distance running and perhaps almost as much during certain times in leadership roles, when I found the need to retreat to a quiet place to reflect on the decisions to be taken. In my later years, the preciousness of time alone for personal reflection has become paramount.

Central to the story of St. Anthony is the legendary and extraordinary supernatural torment he experienced during his sojourns in the desert. In solitude, such experiences can occur.

Many have written on the ascetic, or self-denying, life as epitomized by the desert fathers. One well may ask what St. Anthony was trying to escape, exactly. The precise motivation has been argued by many. My readings suggest that, following the disposal of what may have been considerable property and the resulting provision made to support his sister, he may have been attempting to evade taxes; others have suggested a flight from persecution. It could simply be that Anthony took personally the words of Jesus as recorded in Matthew 19:21: "Jesus answered, 'If you want to be perfect, go, sell your possessions and give to the poor, and you will have treasure in heaven. Then come, follow me.'" There is evidence that earlier pagans also retreated to this ascetic life, which may have provided a model for Anthony's own retreat to the desert.

Certainly, Anthony's life changed dramatically with the loss of both his parents, leaving Anthony and his sister on their own. This development must have brought wrenching, personal soul-searching for Anthony as he ruminated on his responsibility for his sister and his own desire for self-actualization. We learn that Anthony's life was characterized by a series of physical withdrawals. Each of the successive retreats was increasingly remote, during which it appears that considerable hardship was endured.

It occurs to me that there is a link here to our challenges today. We may not literally choose a desert life, but we feel alone, even deserted at times. This can be searing. Take heart: it is a time of growth.

Time Management

Is the investment portfolio that is your business day structured according to your return objectives?

There's a really old joke that goes, "How do you carve a statue of a horse?" The answer, "Chip away all the bits that don't look like a horse." This, of course brings to mind that while there are tasks that can be completed in a day, most jobs are to be executed over time. Generally speaking, each of us has 252 days a year that are available for client-related activities. As a person who has always been a bit of an overachiever, I have constantly thought about how to get the most out of each of those days. I'm also a person that doesn't work well when my desk is cluttered with all the things that I don't need to actually do today!

I am committed to time management. I apportion time for meetings and only expand the time if I am (or can be) convinced that more time is necessary. I start on time; if someone is late their time is reduced or rescheduled. Generally, people become accustomed to my methods fairly quickly.

I take notes! These notes include my confirmation of next steps and timing. Finally, I always have a red letter day circled on my calendar for no more than six weeks ahead—this is a do-nothing-but-relax day.

When short-term investment activities are carefully blended with long-term investment activities, my portfolio return is maximized—and so will yours. OK, time's up!

A Courageous Student

Some years ago, a second-year commerce student knocked on my office door at the university. I had met her once or twice and chatted with her at various functions, but I had never had a deep conversation with her. She sat down and haltingly told me that she had cheated on an exam. I asked her what she was going to do about it. She felt compelled to confess. We talked for a while, and she knew there would be a penalty. Her transgression cost her a lost academic term. For a while I wondered if this might be the last time that I would encounter her. It was not. She returned, completed her studies, and graduated with distinction. Somewhere deep in her a hope welled up, and a new commitment made, together with a completely new sense of who she was. My task was simple—it was to affirm her, and to encourage her. I am so very proud of her.

Soul

The ancient Greeks used the word *pyschi*, which we translate as "soul." I note that the word "soul" appears for the first time in Deuteronomy, the fifth book of the Torah. After this, as will be seen below, we find the word used 129 times and interpreted in numerous ways throughout Scripture. It is presented, for example, as: life, the seat and the inner life of a person in its many and varied aspects, desires, feelings, emotions, and the seat and center of life that transcends our earthly existence. At Deuteronomy 4:29 we find the exhortation, "Seek the LORD your God, and you will find him if you look for him with all your heart and *all your soul*."[51] A number

51. Deut 4:29.

49

of the psalms contain reference to the soul. Psalm 143, for example, offers to us the moving passage, "I spread out my hands to you; my soul thirsts for you like a parched land."[52] Our beloved Psalm 23 includes the passage, "He restores my soul; he guides me in paths of righteousness for his name's sake."[53] The Gospel of Matthew presents Jesus' words, "What good will it be for a man if he gains the whole world, yet forfeits his soul?"[54] There are many wonderful stories that interpret the nature of the soul and its divine relationship. Ronald Rolheiser writes:

> Among the Norwegians there is a beautiful legend, that before a soul is put into the body, that soul is kissed by God, and during all its life on earth, the soul retains a dark, but powerful memory of that kiss and relates everything to it. And then there is the Jewish legend that just before God puts a soul into the body that soul is asked to forget its preternatural life. Hence, just as the soul enters the body, one of God's angels presses the baby's mouth shut, as a gesture that, during its earthly life it is to be silent about its divine origins. The little crevice below each person's nose is the imprint of the angel's forefinger, sealing your lips.[55]

This brings to mind the opening passages of Jeremiah, where we read, "Then the Lord put out his hand and touched my mouth; and the Lord said to me, 'Now I have put words in your mouth.'"[56]

Thomas Oden writes, "Soul, according to its classical Christian conception, is the unitive centre of the inner powers of the person. . . . Soul is that by which we most deeply feel, know and will, and by which the body is animated. The soul lives out of God, and its life transcends this mortal sphere."[57] For me, my soul is the supernatural part of me—that part of me that, if it is healthy, is in

---

52. Ps 143:6.

53. Ps 143:6.

54. Matt 16:26.

55. Rolheiser, *Holy Longing*, 16–17.

56. Jer 1:9.

57. Oden, *Pastoral Theology*, 186.

constant communication with God—even if I am not consciously aware. It is that part of me which is constantly being shaped, formed, and nurtured by the Holy Spirit to guide those intellectual tasks that I am being called to do and for which I am being equipped. My soul is fragile, and succumbs easily to the hurt that it is exposed to. Thus, the caring of souls is, in my view, at the very center of the calling of ministry to another, ensuring that souls are healthy, capable of what Rolheiser describes as, "keeping us energized, vibrant, living with zest and full of hope. . . . Keeping us fixed together."[58]

Caring

Proverbs 1:5 provides the following instruction: "let the wise listen and add to their learning."[59] The prophet Isaiah wrote, "morning by morning he wakens—wakens my ear to listen as those who are taught."[60] Our greatest lesson may be the lesson of paying attention. Jean Stairs writes, "Over and over again, I am struck by the transforming significance of the ministry of listening. . . . Listening for the soul is the primary and essential form our pastoral care takes when we are concerned with fostering spiritual depth in the lives of those within our faith communities."[61]

Caring begins at the moment that we perceive that another person is in need. We choose to move into that place. This may be as simply spending time with another with or without conversation—simply *being*. In Paul's First Letter to Timothy, he writes:

> Until I come, devote yourself to the public reading of Scripture, to preaching and to teaching. Do not neglect your gift, which was given you through a prophetic message when the body of elders laid their hands on you. Be diligent in these matters; give yourself wholly to them, so that everyone may see your progress. Watch your life and

58. Rolheiser, *Holy Longing*, 14.

59. Prov 1:5.

60. Isa 50:4b.

61. Stairs, *Listening for the Soul*, 15.

doctrine closely. Persevere in them, because if you do, you will save both yourself and your hearers.[62]

Interestingly, there is a reflexive element to this passage. Caring for others brings spiritual growth to the person doing the caring. Ballard offers that, "Many modern theologies focus on the importance of lived experience, practice, action and the primacy of human need."[63] When we invite someone to describe a lived experience, a torrent of information is likely to flow. Be ready to receive.

Client Satisfaction

The surprising fact is that many service providers are unaware of the level of satisfaction being experienced among their clients—and this after they expend so much money, time, and talent acquiring those clients. Even if we work hard to ensure that we live up to our commitments, there may be silent relationship-killers undermining our best efforts. For example, there is a very, very high cost of system errors. I learned that something as basic as late delivery of statements can dramatically impact the level of satisfaction that clients experience. This may not seem like much, but I have witnessed in the capital markets industry that dissatisfaction with overall investment performance is frequently not the reason a client moves on; rather it can be disappointment with the administrative aspects of the service delivered.

As your business grows, so does the risk of a wider variation in service delivery experience. Think about your last hotel stay with a brand-name chain. The reputation of the entire chain depends on the single interaction that you had, either in person or not, with one particular staff member.

Here is a simple solution that can actually bring massive unexpected benefits: talk to customers! During my days of growing a business, we advertised that I, as CEO, would be on the client desk

62. 1 Tim 4:13–16.

63. Ballard, "Use of Scripture," 165.

taking calls from 4–7 PM one night a week for clients to reach me if they had any issues to discuss. The astonishing result was this: A few of the calls were from clients wishing to express concern over an unresolved issue, but the greater number were calls from clients giving me suggestions and ideas about products and services. We now had a volunteer marketing department with a vested interest— our clients! Here's the other value that accrued: I was able to interact closely with our client-facing team. I was able to learn from them and to share with them a particular approach to client interaction that I hoped they would emulate. This was a true opportunity not only to lead from alongside, but also to *be* led by our team. The bottom line is that your management style and thoroughness of understanding of the entire value-chain in your organization, whether it is a five-person operation or a major corporation, will become legend, and you will get some great new ideas from your increasingly loyal clients.

This experience led, happily, to another really important decision. During a particular period in the capital markets industry, we had concerns that a large international firm, with significant brand recognition, might enter our market. Our earlier client segmentation work told us to do everything we could do to strengthen our relationship with our greatest revenue-producing clients. First, we created a President's Account for all customers doing above a certain level of trading. They received an unpublished, special-access telephone number that had instant response from our most highly trained trading desk team—these individuals were carefully selected. In addition to this becoming a really appreciated step by our clients, it became valuable internal recognition for the team we chose to work on the President's Desk.

You probably already conduct a client satisfaction survey, but if you don't, start now—put one together as soon as you can to get quantifiable feedback on such areas as your team's apparent ability to perform dependably, accurately, and consistently. Look into your clients' views on service delivery, promptness of delivery, problem resolution, empathy, and, of course, the physical aspects of service, such as readability of statements, etc. You might be amazed at how much dissatisfaction arises from poorly written communications.

Consider surveying 25 percent of your clients every calendar quarter. The finesse of the client experience/productivity equation is achieved through knowing how much the level of service expected is going to cost you, relative to the anticipated revenue. If you can't calculate this, you simply will not know what your profit margin should be. And get down to the detail. Analyze every single client touch point and understand the importance of your approach of each touch point to the client and the cost of providing that touch point: cover mail, electronic, telephone, and face-to-face touch points. I learned many years ago to get into detail on this issue so that I could ensure that we understood the cost and revenue attributable to every action chosen.

These steps may seem unnecessary, but even when the business is small this analysis helps to price elements of your service correctly, and to know when to balance client expectations, competitive offerings, and our own capabilities, resources, and attitudes. Then, you can go out there with confidence, knowing that your clients actually want what you promise, and you will know whether you can deliver on those promises consistently.

By the way, I'm amazed at how many organizations conduct client satisfaction surveys and never review the results. Tie the results of your satisfaction surveys to your client win/loss reports. I have actively tracked and analyzed client win/loss data. It makes a huge difference in awareness of what activities maintain and deepen relationships and revenue. Have a radical focus on monthly activity reports and activity data. Look for warning signs in terms of client usage and get a proactive call/visit plan in place. Create a User Group discussion forum among high users to determine practice suggestions to pass along to other users. The key is to entrench usage as an intentional activity, especially with new users. If you work in an environment that puts its emphasis solely on client acquisition, you may be finding a significant client attrition experience.

Paul K. Bates

A Radical Reliance on Christ

To care for another's soul requires a *radical reliance on Christ*. In my role as a deacon in the Anglican/Episcopal tradition, I bring the weekly Gospel reading to the congregation, and on a roughly monthly basis I am given the opportunity to deliver a sermon. I remember all those years ago now when I prepared to do this for the first time. A colleague of mine reminded me that, in business presentations, people are expecting to hear from me, but in preaching, they might be listening to my words, but it is really God's word that they are focused on. Ever since then, before delivering the Gospel or the message, I stand before the altar for a few minutes and ask God to take over. Michael Knowles brings to us the apostle Paul's perspective on preaching. He writes:

> As (Paul) sees it, preachers provide an example not simply of humility, but of a kind of humiliation and loss that leads them to model radical reliance on Christ. His definition of preaching focuses attention away from the concerns of personality, congregational or denominational identity, or political interest—at least as ends in themselves—and toward the divine mercy that makes ministry possible.[64]

We are provided many more passages in Scripture that affirm the requirement to rely on Christ in our work. These include Jesus' parable of the vine (John 15:1, 4–5), and Jesus' instruction in the Sermon on the Mount (Matt 5:13). The apostle Paul writes, "Follow my example, as I follow the example of Christ."[65] Perhaps the most vivid story of this need for a radical reliance on Christ is presented in Matthew 14. We read:

> But the boat was already a considerable distance from land, buffeted by the waves because the wind was against it. During the fourth watch of the night Jesus went out to them, walking on the lake. When the disciples saw him walking on the lake, they were terrified. "It's a ghost," they said, and cried out in fear. But Jesus immediately said to

64. Knowles, *We Preach Not Ourselves*, 147.
65. 1 Cor 11:1.

55

them: "Take courage! It is I. Don't be afraid." "Lord, if it's you," Peter replied, "tell me to come to you on the water." "Come," he said. Then Peter got down out of the boat, walked on the water and came toward Jesus. But when he saw the wind, he was afraid and, beginning to sink, cried out, "Lord, save me!" Immediately Jesus reached out his hand and caught him. "You of little faith," he said, "why did you doubt?"[66]

This same radical reliance on Christ pervades every element of the caring of souls. In the Anglican/Episcopal tradition, the faithful are invited to the altar rail to receive communion. As a deacon in the church, I participate in the serving of communion, offering the chalice. I continue to witness the powerful impact of the eucharistic celebration. I have seen individuals, couples, mothers, fathers, with their sons and daughters, kneel at the altar rail filled, even overcome, with emotion as they receive the bread and wine.

In Paul's Second Letter to the Corinthians, we find, "but we have this treasure in earthen vessels in order that the surpassing greatness of the power may be of God and not of us."[67] Among other things, Paul is reminding his audience that while our own bodies may decay, it is our spirit—in constant communication with God— that will have constant and renewed strength. Just prior to this, Paul reminds his audience, "For it is God who said, 'Let light shine out of darkness,' who has shone in our hearts to give the light of the knowledge of the glory of God in the face of Jesus Christ."[68] Knowles offers to us that, "Paul's confession amounts to a wry acknowledgement of the scorn with which the [Corinthian] congregation apparently views him. Paul may not look like much, he admits, and his oratory may not be much to write home about (2 Cor. 10:10), but that does not negate his message."[69] In other words, Paul is but a vessel, and a modest one at that, carrying the word of God. Indeed, Jesus also affirms that he is nothing without the Father (cf. John 5:19–20). Purves is instructive in this critical area. He writes:

66. Matt 14:22–33.

67. 2 Cor 4:7.

68. 2 Cor 4:6.

69. Knowles, *We Preach Not Ourselves*, 178.

We should think about ministry as empowerment for faithfulness that God does in and through us, by joining us to the faithfulness of Jesus Christ. Within such empowerment there remains obedience to union with Christ, but obedience is now understood as sharing but the Holy Spirit in Christ's obedience.[70]

We are ordinary people who can do extraordinary things. In the same way that Jesus embodies God's suffering with us (cf. Luke 9:22), so Parker Palmer writes, "To suffer with another person means to be there in whatever way possible, to share the circumstances of the other's life as much as one can—not to add to the world's pool of suffering, but to gain intimate understanding of what the other requires."[71] Phil Zylla points out that, "This notion that God suffers with God's people is rooted in the Exodus. 'The LORD said, I have indeed seen the misery of my people in Egypt. I have heard them crying out because of their slave drivers, and I am concerned about their suffering. So I have come down to rescue them from the hand of the Egyptians' (Exod 3:7–8)."[72]

Central to caring is the theology of suffering, and central to a theology of suffering is a God who suffers with us. Palmer writes, "Only a God who is vulnerable and even needy will evoke our love in a way that completes the circuit of human-and-divine, the circuit in which each of us becomes a carrier of love's energy, a co-creator of the Great Work to be born."[73] In the same way that God is also present in silence, Phil Zylla writes, "There are extended times where words may not be helpful to those who are suffering. Silence is an important call to solidarity with the afflicted."[74]

70. Purves, *Reconstructing Pastoral Theology*, 197.

71. Palmer, *Active Life*, 84.

72. Zylla, *Roots of Sorrow*, 89.

73. Palmer, *Active Life*, 84.

74. Zylla, *Roots of Sorrow*, 88.

Always Believe in the Big Idea

Early in my senior leadership days, I had the privilege of being given permission to launch a brand-new investment product—one that would be a first in our industry. After months of back-testing the concept, working on regulatory approvals, conducting focus groups, and getting buy-in from executive management, the task turned to working with our creative agency to find the right way to introduce the product to the market. When it was all done, and the product went live, I received a framed copy of the first ad from the agency's creative director. The inscription read, "Paul, Always Believe in the Big Idea!" In a way, this celebratory gift inspired me to spend the rest of my career searching for the leading edge of innovation—sometimes with modest and other times with fairly good results.

Living by the Spirit

In Paul's Letter to the Romans we read, "And hope does not disappoint us, because God has poured out his love into our hearts by the Holy Spirit, whom he has given us."[75] Paul uses the term *agape*, thus assuring us that this love is the very nature and essence of God that is brought into the heart in the restorative and regenerative act of soul care. What I am describing here may be the most critical lesson for us in terms of the caring of souls—it is the moment of restoration, of regeneration for the soul. In this essential moment of soul care, the overwhelming love of God can and will reverse the effects of living in the world, wiping away anxiety, sorrow, anger, disappointment, jealousy, even hubris, if our souls can be reoriented and reset. The Gospel of John records Jesus' well-known words following his promise of the Holy Spirit, when he says, "I am the vine. You are the branches. The one remaining in me, this one bears much

75. Rom 5:5.

fruit. Because apart from me you are not able to do anything."[76] By abiding in Christ we bring forth fruit.

The Holy Spirit also brings admonition and reproof, both *to* us, and *through* us, to others. Jesus said, "Be on your guard! If another disciple sins, you must rebuke the offender, and if there is repentance, you must forgive. And if the same person sins against you seven times a day, and turns back to you seven times and says. 'I repent,' you must forgive."[77] Oden presents this passage as Jesus' pattern for Christian counsel. He points out that, "In time, the duty of reproof became connected theologically with the doctrine of sanctification, and practically with the pastoral effort to bring life in Christ to actual fruition. Accordingly, reproof is not something I can charitably withhold from my neighbour."[78] Leviticus 19 presents an extensive list of covenantal accountabilities. Specifically, at Leviticus 19:18a–19, we read, "Rebuke your neighbor frankly so you will not share in his guilt. Do not seek revenge or bear a grudge against one of your people, but love your neighbor as yourself."[79] Indeed, my neighbor owes this same grace to me, as deeply challenging as it can be to accept it. Paul's letter to the Galatians affirms the need to always act with empathy. He writes, "Since we live by the Spirit, let us keep in step with the Spirit. Let us not become conceited, provoking and envying each other."[80]

Business Forecasting

In a start-up venture, from the day I hired our second business development person—the first one being me—trying to forecast business became more complicated. I needed to understand the average cycle time from identifying a potential client, to the reality

---

76. John 15:5.

77. Luke 17:3–4.

78. Oden, *Pastoral Theology,* 207.

79. Lev 19:18a–19.

80. Gal 5:25–26.

of doing business with that client, to the first billing date, was both critical and challenging. Somehow accuracy in expense forecasting is always easier than revenue forecasting. Here's what I learned:

Prospects are suspects until a specific piece of potential business has been identified and discussed. Contacts are not suspects until there has been a follow-up call or meeting following the date of first contact. No one is a prospect until a specific proposal has been made. And here's the most amazing reality—a really large number of contacts are never followed up on in order to discover potential business opportunities.

Detailed and accurate call reports are critical to forecasting, and the reality is that this is a truly task-oriented management function. Yes, a spreadsheet is required, with columns for contacts, suspects, prospects, proposals, follow-up, and a report of closed, or lost, business. If a name stays in the contact column for more than two call reports, that name should probably be discounted. The same rule holds true for suspects. Things only get interesting from a revenue forecasting perspective when we reach the prospect column. Closeable business, and the timing and quantum of that business, can then enter the realm of meaningful analysis. These activities are at the heart of activities management. Without these activities, all you have is a wish list.

All this means that the heart of successful business forecasting is the same as it has always been—in-depth analysis of, and dialogue about, the business-development pipeline, combined with frank and rational discussion of probable business and the timing of that business. Finally, all those contacts that do not result in closed business should be kept. Circumstances change, and periodic follow-up will always result in fresh potential.

Moving this concept up one level, having a realistic understanding of how long it will take for a new addition to your team to reach revenue production maturity is also critical. This is very much dependent on the experience and network of the person coming on board, and the norms within your particular sector of business. A colleague of mine used the paradigm that it would take, on average, four full quarters of activity for a newly hired person, even one with experience, to reach revenue production maturity.

So, here's a goal: To become as accurate, over a quarterly cycle, with your revenue forecasting as you are with your expense forecasting.

How to Get Ahead

How to get ahead *without worrying about how to get ahead*. Some years ago, a person, early in their first management role, would regularly come to my office to ask when they might receive a promotion (and a raise in pay). The challenge was that they never offered any particular rationale for the request, other than stating something like, "I think it's time!" Sadly, this person never received the promotion that they so eagerly sought.

I tried to give the advice that a boss of mine had given me decades before. That advice is that career opportunities frequently come faster than we are actually ready for them. In other words, stop fixating on getting the next opportunity, and focus on being *ready* for it. Here's the mantra that I often gave to business students: Get to work early, learn everything; stay until the work is done.

True Leadership

Sara Parkin writes, "A leader is a post-holder and may be elected, chosen or appointed to lead something. . . . *Leadership* may be exercised by anyone. From anywhere in an organization or group. Even when an appointed leader exists, others may exercise leadership."[81]

The great reality is that true leadership is in very short supply. Your constant application to the work at hand, combined with your constant preparation for the work ahead, is going to be noticed. You will be raised up through the organization faster than you think, and you will be ready. I might add also that we all need you more than ever."

81. Parkin, *Positive Deviant*, 94 (emphasis mine).

Surrender

James Loder writes that in the moment of surrender we are, "known, seen and authorized (by God)."[82] Loder describes Paul's experience on the road to Damascus as such an event. He writes, "Not only is Saul, seen, known and understood, he is authorized; first by this direct meeting and later by confirming events . . . called into the making of history."[83] In Paul's conversion, God calls upon one individual, a disciple named Ananias, who is to play a major pastoral role. It is immediately important to note here that God calls upon Ananias to provide both spiritual and physical solace to Saul. The Acts of the Apostles records that, "Now there was a disciple named Ananias. The Lord said to him in a vision, 'Ananias.' He answered, 'Here I am Lord.' The Lord said to him, 'Get up and go to the street called Straight, and at the house of Judas look for a man of Tarsus named Saul. At this moment he is praying."[84] So it is that this is a critical time for spiritual guidance. The calling of Paul is narrated three times in Acts (chs. 9, 12, and 16). In Galatians 1, he asserts, "the gospel that was proclaimed by me is not of human origin,"[85]

While Paul does not mention Ananias, Stan Lundgren asserts:

> It is remarkable that Luke is very careful in describing the function of Ananias in the narrative of Paul's calling. . . . Luke describes in Acts 9:12 and 9:17–18 what Ananias has to do. In a dream the Lord tells Ananias to go to Paul. The Lord relates how Paul has seen Ananias entering the house and laying on his hands 'so that he might regain his sight' (Acts 9:12). In Acts 9:17 Ananias himself presents his own function. He announces to Saul that he is sent by the Lord 'that you may regain your sight and be filled with the Holy Spirit.' Ananias has a strictly limited task in the story of Paul's calling. He shall heal and baptize Paul. This is his active role.[86]

82. Loder, *Transforming Moment*, 22.

83. Loder, *Transforming Moment*, 22.

84. Acts 9:10–12.

85. Gal 1:11b.

86. Lundgren, "Ananias," 120.

Lundgren also points to an additional role for Ananias. He states, "The other function was to serve as a witness to the fact that Paul was called without mediation of man and that he in fact had his mandate from the Lord."[87]

This narrative may well present Ananias as the archetype for the caring role of coming alongside those who are struggling with their faith—not to mediate, but simply to be a vessel through which Christ, through the Holy Spirit, brings God's love and mercy.

I suspect that in our collective experiences we would concur that for many this struggle can be significant, if not monumental. Before we can reach intimacy with God, and indeed greater intimacy with another person, we must first find stillness in solitude, which becomes a path to prayer. However, the silence that is the prelude to solitude may be the most significant threshold to cross. Louis Brodie draws us to two recurring Genesis themes present in Jacob's struggle (Gen 32:22–32). One theme is, "The image of working purposefully in the dark . . . seen as reshaping of the prophetic words which have the effect of encouraging people to struggle through their national nightmare."[88] The other theme is, "Man's (sic) fundamental struggle with sin and a superhuman adversary."[89] For one who has not yet accepted faith, indeed, even for those who have accepted faith, to ask them to be still, to enter solitude, can be a daunting request. Moreover, many will actively resist such an imperative.

We avoid silence out of fear of the darkness of our existence, and out of fear of a struggle with the errors of our past. In silence and darkness these errors seem to grow to superhuman proportions (as with Jacob) and we are afraid that they will fell our spirit. We can imagine how profoundly difficult it might be to contemplate devoting time to silence, without distractions, without the glittering lights of computer screens, mobile devices, televisions, etc., in order to enter into solitude. To say the least, it can be painful to confront perceived missed opportunities. We may even feel that it is too late—we

87. Lundgren, "Ananias," 122.

88. Brodie, "Jacob's Travail," 48.

89. Brodie, "Jacob's Travail," 31.

have too much baggage—to contemplate a relationship with the divine. Loneliness can be completely debilitating. Harry Sullivan writes that, "Loneliness in itself is more terrible than anxiety."[90]

Being transformed into a person that is in communion with the Holy Trinity makes possible a deeper intimacy with others; it is the removal of the fear of such intimacy. Nouwen writes, "Contemplative Prayer often brings us to an intimate encounter with the love of God, revealed in Jesus. In such an experience we come to know even more deeply that God is not against us, but for us; not far from us, but with us; not outside of us, but deeply within us."[91] The Psalmist writes, "The Lord is my light and my salvation; whom shall I fear?"[92] Nouwen asserts that, "Fear is the great enemy of intimacy."[93] For many, liminal moments hold both anticipation and trepidation. Our call is to step into the companionship role at this moment. We affirm our solidarity, through our presence, comfort, and action. As Nouwen states, "Solidarity is the other side of intimacy."[94]

Communion

Communion—intimacy with God's love—becomes the foundation for a morality that is humble—a morality that puts us in harmony with all of creation. Florence Bourg writes:

> Dennis Billy's essay, 'Moral Mysticism in a Parish Setting,' presumes every Christian should be a mystic. 'Mysticism' is defined not by ecstatic experience of God in this life—something accessible to relatively few, but as a deepening awareness of one's Christian vocation, something to which all people are called.' Billy uses the qualifier 'moral mysticism' to stress that Christian mysticism not only yields altered states of consciousness, but drives us 'to

90. Sullivan, *Interpersonal Theory of Personality*, 262.

91. Nouwen, *Spiritual Formation*, 12.

92. Ps 27:1a.

93. Nouwen, *Lifesigns*, 18.

94. Nouwen, *Lifesigns*, 30.

actively pursue personal and/or social commitments of a loving (and therefore moral) nature."[95]

This perspective would resonate with Nouwen's view and puts into context Nouwen's assertion, "The spiritual life has to do with the heart of existence. This is a good word. By heart I do not mean the seat of our feelings as opposed to the seat of our thoughts; I mean the center of our being; that place where we are most ourselves; where we are most human."[96] This is underscored also by Paul Mickey, who writes, "The pastor's relationship to people is not to be seen as one of a perfect moral influence, but it is a two-way relationship in which the resources of the 'imperfect' pastor are immediately and continually available to imperfect and incomplete people."[97] Thus morality and caring are inextricable—both constitute the pastoral relationship. Noddings underscores this when she asserts that, "Moral behavior arises out of our natural impulse to care."[98] We may not all, literally, be pastors, but we can be companions. I spoke earlier about Ananias. As far as we know, he held no priestly title. He was prepared, he was called, he responded.

Am I Worthy of Love?

We ask a significant question: Am I worthy of love? Are others capable of loving me? This deeply personal, fundamental, and perhaps fearful question may be emblematic of the threshold moment between silence and solitude, when we may ask, "Is anything worth it?" It represents a central element of the fear of intimacy. John the apostle makes it clear:

> And so we know and rely on the love God has for us. God is love. Whoever lives in love lives in God, and God in him. In this way, love is made complete among us so that

95. Bourg, "Spirituality and Moral Theology," 130.
96. Nouwen, *Letters to Marc about Jesus*, 5.
97. Mickey, "Is There a 'Theology?,'" 30.
98. Noddings, *Caring*, 51

we will have confidence on the Day of Judgment, because in this world we are like him. There is no fear in love. But perfect love drives out fear, because fear has to do with punishment. The one who fears is not made perfect in love. We love because he first loved us.[99]

When we accept Christ, we are miraculously, automatically, fully enfolded in his love. When we are drawn into a caring relationship with another, we are effectively entering holy ground. John Patton speaks of a relationship beyond words when he writes of a, "wholeness that exceeds what can be known, done and said."[100]

Vocation

Getting on to the right path, especially as we reach midlife, may have a great deal to do with forming a crystallized picture of one's legacy. This is finding purpose beyond the immediate, it is accepting our divine vocation. This may be a call to uproot. It may be a call to do the same work. Ronald Rolheiser makes the statement, "Spirituality is about what we do with the fire inside us."[101] In other words, we accept Christ as the source of our future. This is the movement into prayer. Nouwen writes, "Prayer is being unbusy with God instead of being busy with other things. Prayer is primarily to do nothing useful or productive in the presence of God."[102] This is a sea-change demand. Nouwen also calls for a movement from resentment to gratitude. He writes, "Gratitude is more than an occasional 'thanks be to God.' Gratitude is the attitude that enables us to let go of anger (and) receive the hidden gifts of those we want to serve."[103] This is letting go of anger—anger toward others and toward ourselves. Kathryn M. Gow writes, "It is relatively easy to accept that people

99. 1 John 4:16–19.

100. Patton, *From Ministry to Theology*, 73.

101. Rolheiser, *Holy Longing*, 11.

102. Nouwen, *Spiritual Formation*, 19.

103. Nouwen, *Spiritual Formation*, 63.

must release negative emotions in order to heal. . . . Emotional detachment is not about suppression or repression of emotions, but about freedom from the tyranny and bondage of emotions."[104] Ultimately, Nouwen calls for a movement from fear to love. He writes, "When we begin to understand at a deep, spiritual level that we live surrounded by love in communion with God no matter what the external circumstances, we can let go of the fear that lurks on the outskirts of our minds."[105] To be intimate with another is to have overcome fear.

And This from My Sister

At a school assembly (as deputy headmaster) I took in a bag of potatoes, each with the name of someone who had done me wrong written in felt pen. For example, the pop singer who earned me a detention in 1969! (Allegedly I'd written his name on a desk; I hadn't.) I gave each one to a student to hold for me, and told the stories. They would gasp with horror at the unfairness of each situation that I described. But then I noticed my bag was empty, no longer heavy for me to carry around with me every day, no longer full of slightly rancid-smelling old potatoes—it was time to let go of all that trouble.

Magpies in Dublin

During a visit to Dublin, Ireland, there was a wedding at the hotel where I was staying. Watching the guests gathering in the gardens outside, I noticed a couple of magpies scavenging. Looking it up, I found that the magpie is considered one of the most intelligent nonmammalians—able to recognize itself in a mirror. Watching them brought to mind Jesus' Sermon on the Mount:

104. Gow, "Letting Go," 162.
105. Nouwen, *Spiritual Formation*, 79.

Look at the birds of the air: they neither sow nor reap nor gather into barns, and yet your heavenly father feeds them. Are you not of more value than they? And can any of you by worrying add a single hour to your span of life?[106]

John 16:13 reads, "When the Spirit of truth comes, he will guide you into all the truth; for he will not speak on his own, but will speak whatever he hears, and he will declare to you the things that are to come."

Truth and Reconciliation

As I finish this work, I have on my desk a small stone on which is written the name of a missing indigenous woman, age undocumented.

I understand that bearing witness to truth is a critical step in the path to reconciliation. Deena Klodt has explained to me that the teaching of the Two Row Wampum Treaty boils down to the spirit of relationship: peace, respect, and friendship. May God lead us, in courage, to find one another, see one another, and to uphold this together. It's time.

106. Matt 6:26–27.

Your Turn

How about you? The following question-starters are provided to perhaps get you thinking about a few things.

- Jesus said, "Enter through the narrow gate; for the gate is wide and the road is easy that leads to destruction, and there are many who take it. For the gate is narrow and the road is hard that leads to life, and there are few who find it."[107] How will you find the narrow gate?

- I have said that "God has many elbows." These elbows were attached to the arms of people that I encountered at critical moments in my own faith journey who nudged me along—asking me questions, making suggestions. Are there such people in your orbit now also?

- I have come to believe that God anticipates our actions and is at work in our lives: encouraging us, patiently forgiving our shortcomings, and celebrating our journey toward him. How do you feel about this?

- In Matthew 5:16 we read, "Let your light shine before others in such a way that they may see your good works and glorify your Father who is in Heaven." Paradoxically, I suggest that this requires us to become small. What do you think about this?

- Work is complex. It can also be a completely performance-driven and sometimes cynical environment. How do you cope with this?

107. Matt 7: 13–14.

- In work, we are given the opportunity to model virtuous behavior. Does someone come to mind who is such a model for you?

- We will be remembered for how we conduct ourselves in times of transition and upheaval. Your thoughts?

- There is an expression, "Of the person to whom much is given, much is expected." Your thoughts?

- When you witness bullying or intimidating behavior, what is your response?

- We can think of the word "legacy" as sending the product of our labor on to the future—a future beyond our earthly lives. What do you think about this?

- When we rise up against greed, and when we follow the call to feed the hungry, clothe the naked, and shelter the homeless, we are participating in God's struggle against chaos. What do you think about this statement?

About the Author

The Reverend Deacon Dr. Paul K. Bates, MTS, DPT, FCPA, FCMA, CMC

Paul holds a Doctorate in Practical Theology (DPT) from McMaster Divinity College in Ontario, Canada. He is a Chartered Professional Accountant (FCPA), Fellow of the Society of Management Accountants (FCMA) and Certified Management Consultant (CMC). Now semi-retired, Paul is focused on a portfolio of graduate-level teaching, governance, and consulting in corporate, government, and regulatory roles, together with community service as a deacon in his church, following a career that has included senior academic administration, extensive lecturing (undergraduate, graduate, and executive education), investor advocacy, capital markets regulation, and broad corporate and not-for-profit service (public and private).

Paul is a published author of peer-reviewed academic journal articles as well as works in the academic and popular press. His most recent work is *For Others to Follow: An Ethos of Leadership Grounded in Faith* (Wipf and Stock).

Bibliography

Ballard, Paul. "The Use of Scripture." In *Practical Theology*, edited by Bonnie J. Miller-McLemore, 163–75. Malden MA: Wiley, 2014.

Barton, Ruth H. *Strengthening the Soul of Your Leadership*. Westmont, IL: Intervarsity, 2008.

Bates, Paul K. "The Corporation with Integrity: A Well-Found Vessel in an Angry Sea." *Executive Action* (May 2009) 1–3.

———. "Paracletic Ministry: A Study in Pastoral Encounters with Male Mid-Career Spiritual Searchers." *Practical Theology* 10.1(March 2017) 1–14.

Best, Patricia. "Born Again on Bay Street: Patricia Best on Why the Suits are Turning to God." *Toronto Life* (November 2001) 69–72.

Bourg, Florence. "Spirituality and Moral Theology: Essays from a Pastoral Perspective (Review)." *Spiritus* 2:1 (2002) 129–32.

"BP CEO Apologizes for 'Thoughtless' Oil Spill Comment." *Reuters*, June 2, 2010. https://www.reuters.com/article/us-oil-spill-bp-apology-idUSTRE6515NQ20100602.

Brodie, Louis T. "Jacob's Travail and Jacob's Struggle: A Test Case for Measuring the Influence of the Book of Jeremiah on the Present Text of Genesis." *Journal for the Study of the Old Testament* 19 (1981) 31–60.

Buber, Martin. *I and Thou*. New York: Simon & Schuster, 1996.

Collins, Kenneth J. *The Theology of John Wesley: Holy Love and the Shape of Grace*. Nashville: Abingdon, 2007.

deSilva, David. *An Introduction to the New Testament: Contexts, Methods and Ministry Formation*. Ashland, OR: Blackstone, 2004.

Dryden, J. De Waal. "Revisiting Romans 7: Law, Self, and Spirit." *Journal for the Study of Paul and His Letters* 5.1 (2015) 129–51.

Eliot, T. S. *The Waste Land and Other Poems*. London: Faber and Faber, 1952.

Farrokhzad, Forugh. "The Wind Will Carry Us in My Night so Brief." https://www.goodreads.com/quotes/7268595-the-wind-will-carry-us-in-my-night-so-brief.

Gow, Kathryn M. "Letting Go: For Physical, Emotional, and Spiritual Health." *Journal of Religion and Health* 38.2 (1999) 155–65.

Gowan, Donald E. *Eschatology in the Old Testament*. Philadelphia: Fortress, 1986.

Bibliography

Haga, Susan, and Mary Carouba. *Women at Ground Zero*. Indianapolis: Alpha, 2002.

Hall, Thelma, *Too Deep for Words: Rediscovering Lectio Divina*. New York: Paulist, 1988.

Herring, Cedric. "Does Diversity Pay?: Race, Gender, and the Business Case for Diversity." *America Sociological Association* 74.2 (April 2009) 208–24.

Knowles, Michael, P. *Of Seeds and the People of God*. Eugene, OR: Cascade, 2015.

———. *We Preach Not Ourselves: Paul on Proclamation*. Grand Rapids: Brazos, 2008.

Loder, James. *The Transforming Moment*. 2nd ed. Colorado Springs: Helmers and Howard, 1989.

Lombard, Jay. *The Mind of God: Neuroscience, Faith, and a Search for the Soul*. New York: Harmony, 2017.

Lundgren, Sten. "Ananias and the Calling of Paul in Acts." *Studia Theologica— Nordic Journal of Theology* 25:1 (1971) 117–22.

Mickey, Paul, A. "Is There a 'Theology' in Seward Hiltner's Pastoral Theology?" *Pastoral Theology* 21:8 (1970) 27–32.

Noddings, Nel. *Caring: A Feminine Approach to Ethics and Moral Education*. 2nd ed. Berkeley: University of California, 2003.

Nouwen, Henri J. *Letters to Marc about Jesus: Living a Spiritual Life in a Material World*. New York: Harper Collins, 1988.

———. *Lifesigns: Intimacy, Fecundity and Ecstasy in Christian Perspective*. New York: Doubleday, 1966.

———. *Spiritual Formation: Following the Movements of the Spirit*. New York: Doubleday, 1966.

Oden, Thomas C. *Pastoral Theology: Essentials of Ministry*. New York: Harper Collins, 1983.

Palmer, Parker J. *The Active Life: A Spirituality of Work, Creativity and Caring*. San Francisco: Wiley, 1990.

Parkin, Sara. *The Positive Deviant: Sustainability Leadership in a Perverse World*. London: Earthscan, 2010.

Patton, John. *From Ministry to Theology: Pastoral Action and Reflection*. Nashville: Abingdon, 1990.

———. "Physicians of the Soul." In *Turning Points in Pastoral Care*, edited by Leroy Aden and J. Harold Ellens, 159–72. Grand Rapids: Baker, 1990.

Pennington, Jonathan T. *The Sermon on the Mount and Human Flourishing: A Theological Commentary*. Grand Rapids: Baker Academic, 2017.

Purves, Andrew. *Reconstructing Pastoral Theology in the Classical Tradition*. Louisville: Westminster John Knox, 2001.

Rock, David, and Heidi Grant. "Diverse Teams Feel Less Comfortable—And That's Why They Perform Better." *Harvard Business Review*, November 4, 2016. https://hbr.org/2016/11/why-diverse-teams-are-smarter .

Rolheiser, Ronald. *The Holy Longing: The Search for a Christian Spirituality*. New York: Doubleday, 1999.

Bibliography

Stairs, Jean. *Listening for the Soul: Pastoral Care and Spiritual Direction.* Minneapolis: Fortress, 2000.

Sullivan, Henry Stack. *The Interpersonal Theory of Personality.* New York: Norton, 1953.

Tolkien, J. R. R. *The Fellowship of the Ring.* London: HarperCollins, 1993.

Webster's New World College Dictionary. 4th ed. New York: MacMillan, 1999.

Widdicombe, Tom. *Be with Your Horse: Getting to the Heart of Horsemanship.* Exeter, UK: David & Charles, 2005.

Wyszynski, Stefan. *All You Who Labor: Work and the Sanctification of Daily Life.* Manchester, NH: Sophia Institute, 1995.

Zylla, Phil C. *The Roots of Sorrow: A Pastoral Theology of Suffering.* Waco, TX: Baylor University, 2012.

www.ingramcontent.com/pod-product-compliance
Lightning Source LLC
Chambersburg PA
CBHW060425090426
42734CB00011B/2450